Arthur B. Toan, Jr., C.P.A., is Partner in charge of Management Advisory Services for Price Waterhouse & Co. He is a member of the Management Services Committee and Chairman of the Committee on Electronic Computers of the American Institute of Certified Public Accountants and serves on the Planning Council of the American Management Association. Mr. Toan has written widely for the professional journals on management services, operations research, and other accounting and management topics.

USING INFORMATION TO MANAGE

Arthur B. Toan, Jr., C.P.A.

PARTNER, PRICE WATERHOUSE & CO.

THE RONALD PRESS COMPANY • NEW YORK

109784

658.4
T 627

Copyright © 1968 by
THE RONALD PRESS COMPANY

———

All Rights Reserved

No part of this book may be reproduced
in any form without permission in writing
from the publisher.

Library of Congress Catalog Card Number: 68–28846

PRINTED IN THE UNITED STATES OF AMERICA

Preface

This is a book about information and its role in the management process—its strengths, its limitations, and the legitimate expectations an executive can have as to the support that information can provide.

Information clearly is inseparable from the management process. One can, in fact, contend that it is the life blood of management, for none of the significant elements of running a business—planning, organizing, operating, or controlling—can exist in a practical sense without it. Information helps provide the answers to two basic questions—"How am I doing?" and "Where am I going?"—and a number of significant secondary questions with which every executive must be concerned.

It is equally obvious that information is not and cannot be a substitute for management itself.

The information needs of various organizations differ and yet have a good deal in common. They differ because organizations' missions are different; their sizes, methods of organization, geographical dispersion, and technical specialization vary; their stages of development are not the same. There are many other reasons. At the same time, management needs for information have much in common because, while the emphasis on and techniques for obtaining information may vary, the underlying questions that must be answered are essentially the same. Within reasonable limits one can contend that while information may differ in order and complexity between the great and the small, the worldwide and the local, the commercial and the governmental, it is all essentially similar in purpose and in kind.

This book deals with the twin questions of how to use information to stay out of trouble and how to use information to

iii

analyze troublesome situations as part of effecting a cure. It shows how to use information to define positive goals and move toward them with greater assurance. The need to establish the desired level of information detail and degree of accuracy is emphasized throughout.

The business of modest size and its executives have been used as a frame of reference in order to simplify the process of setting forth management problems and the role of information in helping to solve them, but most of what is said has wide application. The book concludes with a discussion of the impact of three increasingly important factors—computers, mathematical techniques, and the heightened emphasis on planning.

In the last analysis, the usefulness of information is a function of its quantity, quality, and intrinsic suitability and of the executive's willingness and ability to use what he receives. It is hoped that this book, by dealing with both aspects of the question, will help to ensure that information fills its role in helping the business executive to practice more effectively the none-too-simple art of directing his enterprise toward the goals he has set for it.

ARTHUR B. TOAN, JR.

New York, New York
April, 1968

Contents

1 Looking at Current Results **3**

The Dangers of Success · Uses of Current Information · Requirements of Good Information · An Approach to Information on Current Results

2 Planning and Budgeting **19**

Planning and the Maturing Enterprise · What Planning Really Means · Forces Affecting the Future · How Planning Is Done · Central Role of Information

3 Costs, Prices, and Profits **31**

A Declining-Profit Problem · Special Cost and Profit Analyses · Using Cost and Profit Analyses · Reports Most Frequently Found Useful · Benefits of Cost, Price, and Profit Information

4 Markets, Customers, and Products . . . **52**

The Static Sales-Curve Problem · Sources of Available Market and Product Information · Obtaining the Information · Evaluating and Using the Information

5 Inventory and Production Management . . **67**

Functions of Inventories · Information Most Useful in Managing Inventories · Areas of Operating Performance Improved by Good Inventory Management

v

6 Cash Management   84

Key Problems in Managing Cash · Putting the Cash Plan
Together · Comparing Actual Performance with the
Plan · How to Use Information in Cash Planning

7 Delegation and Control   101

Delegation of Responsibilities · Basic Approaches to
Delegation · The Enabling Role of Information · Establishing a Chain of Command · Freedom to Manage

8 New Forces Affecting the Role of Information   111

Electronic Computers and Communications Equipment ·
Operations Research · Emphasis on Planning and the Decision-Making Process · Dual Role of Information

9 Evaluating a Management Information System   131

Symptoms of Inadequate Information · Inspection of the
Information System

Glossary of Business and Information Terms   .   143

Index   149

USING INFORMATION TO MANAGE

1

Looking at Current Results

THE DANGERS OF SUCCESS

Walter Lawson, president and part owner of Appliance Components, Inc., was enjoying two of the problems of success—a thriving business and a well-educated son finishing his first year in the company after graduation from business school.

"It's hard to imagine," said Mr. Lawson, "that a whole year has gone by since your graduation. Needless to say it has been a very pleasant year for me, having you working for Appliance, and I think a very good thing for the company, too. I've grown very fond of this company and proud of what I think we've done—rapid growth, good profits, good morale, and a respected place in the community. I know, of course, that we can do better, and I hope that we will. You must have a point of view about the company based upon your educational experience and your relative newness here. If you had to pick an area in which you think we are seriously weak, what would you think it might be?"

"This is a successful company, all right," was the reply. "It has good products, good people, a good reputation, and a real sense of purpose. You've done a lot since you've become president, and I expect you'll do more. If I have one concern, though, it is that we run the danger of moving ahead of our ability to manage the company—with more products, more people, more customers, more locations, and so on, than we can handle—and that we may wake up some day and find that things have gotten out of control. I just don't think we know enough about how well or how poorly we are doing, and I don't think we know it soon enough.

"Several things have led me to this conclusion. First, I don't find the kind of information coming to you and the rest of management that I had been taught to expect. Second, I notice that you and the other officers don't know the answers to a lot of questions that I think you should. Last, and this is what has made the biggest impression, it seems to me that some of the other companies in this town have gotten themselves into serious difficulties—in part, at least, because they didn't know how they were doing in time to take action to correct their deficiencies. For example, Atlas Farm Equipment seems to have gotten itself into an awful cash position because it didn't know its receivables collections were slowing down. Mr. Black's company seems to have unintentionally spent a lot of money acquiring equipment to produce its least profitable line of products. And James Manufacturing, while maybe it shouldn't have been trying to take on more complex products anyway, certainly didn't have the information to show how serious things were or to do something about them in order to save the situation. I really think we should spend some more effort so that we know more about what's going on."

Lawson thought for a minute. "If you had said this a year ago, I think the impression you would have made on me would have been just about zero. Now, quite frankly, it isn't. I can see just enough chance for me to make the same mistakes as Atlas and Black and James to feel that I need something more than I have. I can see that if we continue to grow, the situation gets more complicated, not less. What you say makes a good deal of sense. We really do have to do an awful lot of guessing and assuming about how we stand, and about many more things than we did when we were small. There is a greater risk involved in this than I think I realized. Let's try to do something constructive in this area this year."

USES OF CURRENT INFORMATION

What is the purpose of such information? What can a president like Lawson hope to get from information about how he stands? An executive can expect four things:

1. A better, more factual basis on which to make decisions on short-term actions and longer-range plans.
2. A better and faster indication of when things are not going right.
3. A stimulus to take action when it should be taken, and a better basis for deciding what should be done.
4. An incentive for making better plans.

Information should increase the president's ability to discipline and spur his business and thus to guide it rather than to let it drift. It is, for example, a rare businessman who, without knowing whether his unit production costs are good or poor, can sustain the same high degree of interest in controlling or reducing them as can one who receives this information. It is a rare executive who can feel comfortable or unconcerned or refuse to take action when this information turns out to be bad.

Information showing "how I am doing" should help to indicate how good the policies, plans, decisions, and actions really are in the face of the specific business situation with which the executive is dealing, and should indicate whether they should be retained or changed in order to be more effective in the future. The driver who has the wheel of an automobile never ceases to use information about how he is doing to evaluate the soundness of his actions; the control system used to aim the rocket fired from an airplane constantly uses information fed back to it to adjust the direction of the gun from which the rocket will be fired. If an executive is to accomplish the comparable business purpose, he must constantly use the feedback he gets from the information he receives. If he lacks the information or if it fails him because it is unreliable, incomplete, or too late, he will have trouble in guiding the business entrusted to him.

Knowledge of the current situation should tell the executive what resources and obligations he has, how these resources are committed by existing obligations or plans, and, to a great degree, what freedom of action is now open to him. A statement of "how we stand," more often than one would like to think, tells a businessman what must be improved for his business to become healthy again. Like a snapshot at a given point of time, it freezes the business so that its health can be determined and the diverse elements of the company—cash, accounts receivable, inventories, plant and equipment, liabilities, and shareholders' equity—can be seen in proper perspective.

Knowledge of current results should provide one of the vital motivations for planning. Without a knowledge of how the company has done and is currently doing, businessmen will find little reason or purpose in planning what should be done in the future. If a businessman carefully prepares a plan but never has much notion about how it works out, except perhaps long after the fact, a very important part of the process of management will seem theoretical and unreal and will soon fall into disuse.

REQUIREMENTS OF GOOD INFORMATION

About a month later, after Lawson had discussed his conversation with his son with several of the other company executives, the group met to listen to the younger Lawson's ideas.

"When I started to look around, I found out there was plenty of information. The difficulty seemed to be that it was fragmented and uncoordinated. We almost seemed to know more about the parts than about the whole. For instance, I noticed that while Dad was gone the following items arrived on his desk: the last two weeks' payroll totals, a corrected copy of the last quarter's financial statements, a summary of last month's shipments, the last two weeks' production reports, several memorandums discussing reactions to products that had been recently introduced, credit reports on several customers, several trade journals, a couple of economic studies, and a host of miscellaneous pieces of information. Much of it was unorganized, out of context, or otherwise not at all easy to put into focus.

"The trick, I decided, was to figure out what information was really useful and to exclude that which was not. After considerable thought, I decided to use certain criteria. I decided that information would be most useful when it (1) dealt with the vital aspects of the business; (2) was sufficiently reliable to serve its purpose; (3) reached us soon enough to enable us to act; (4) came to us in an understandable form; and (5) was accompanied by an appropriate basis of comparison.

"I also concluded the opposite: that if the information seriously failed these five tests, it would probably be far less valuable—maybe even downright dangerous to rely on."

Significance and Vitality

The first requirements of good information are significance and vitality. If information is to be significant, it must deal with those aspects of a business about which important decisions are to be made or important actions taken. It must not deal with the trivial and the unimportant. Whether the items it deals with are specific or general is not particularly significant. What counts is that important problems, opportunities, and/or decisions are involved.

What is important for one business or industry will not always be important for another. What is vital at one stage of a company's career or under one set of conditions often will differ from what is important at another.

For example, when Lawson was struggling to get Appliance Components started, he was primarily interested in making the company a going concern. To do this he needed to develop a reliable product, obtain sales, and raise enough cash to finance his start-up costs. Profits would have been nice, but he did not consider them essential, although he well knew he could not stand a substantial loss. Getting started was essential, and he needed information relevant to that purpose.

Now, six years later, the company was growing rapidly and its needs had shifted. Growth had led to capacity problems. The executives needed to keep a closer eye on current and predicted sales levels. Growth had tied up a lot of capital. Therefore, there was a need to watch inventories, receivables, and cash more closely. Now that the company was established, the officers and shareholders wanted it to be more profitable. This required a closer look at costs and profits than was necessary six years before, when costs and profits were of relatively less concern than getting sales and learning to manufacture a reliable product. Finally, growth had brought with it a more complex business, which was more difficult to manage and which required that greater attention be paid to its overall health.

What is significant and vital information to Lawson will reflect the kind of company he runs. It is a mixture of what is immediately necessary to manage the business today and what is necessary to measure how well the company is moving toward both its short- and its long-term goals. It is a mixture that spotlights a small area of the business and that provides a view of a broad area of the business or the business as a whole.

Reliability

The next criterion is reliability. Reliability is first a matter of good records and procedures, of good basic data accurately recorded and summarized in meaningful reports. It is a matter of how effectively the system and methods, the mechanical aids and the supervision, and the controls operate to assure that data will be completely, promptly, and properly reported and recorded. It is the result of methods and practices that assure that what has taken place is appropriately summarized in reports that management can understand and use.

Reliability is also a matter of accuracy. Accuracy does not mean 100 per cent accuracy, for often this is either not possible or not worth the time or cost. The accuracy should be sufficient to serve its purpose. For example, when one wishes to find out the age of the accounts receivable, one need only know that $100,000 of accounts receivable are outstanding and that about 25 per cent are past due by a month, 15 per cent by two months, and 3 per cent by a longer period. Reliability does not require a statement that the amounts are $104,904.59, $26,966.18, $15,434.21, and $2,992.46, respectively. Each piece of information has a permissible margin of error that is determined by its purpose. Some margins must be very small; others can be quite large.

Reliability, finally, is the result of using sound principles to develop the information itself, for, if the basis on which the information was compiled is unsound, no amount of "accuracy" can correct that fact. An unfortunate fact of life is that, even when an executive receives the right kind of information, it can be misleading or wrong.

Part of the problem may be basic errors in the records themselves, such as an arithmetic error in assigning manufacturing overhead to inventory. It is more likely, however, that the problem is the result of deficiencies in the way the records are kept. For example, interim inventory values and cost of goods sold figures may be of dubious validity because some inventory withdrawals have not been recorded or unit manufacturing costs are not known; the adequacy of reserves may not have been reviewed; management-owners often do not pay themselves realistic salaries; unsound principles may have been applied; or "apples and oranges," such as production and administrative overheads, may be so badly intermingled that one can tell only about the business as a whole, rather than about its component parts. In short, the information produced can be what was intended, but what was intended can be unsound or inadequate.

Timeliness

Good information requires timeliness: the information must be available soon enough to make a decision and to take action in advance of or soon after it is found to be necessary.

The need for timeliness obviously varies with the nature of the information. For example, in most businesses a knowledge of orders undelivered past the promised date or items out of stock should be made available more rapidly than a knowledge of profits for the period; cash balances should be known more quickly than the amount of money invested in plant.

One of the reasons for thinking about timeliness or speed—and reliability or accuracy, too, for that matter—is that these factors are rather directly related to cost: increases in speed and accuracy often bring a more than equal increase in cost. At times a reduction in accuracy—as by the use of estimates or approximations—may be a way to achieve the desired speed without increases in costs. Another way may be to construct the records themselves so that the information is simultaneously prepared as a by-product or co-product of maintaining them.

At any rate, a proper balance of speed, cost, and accuracy clearly should be attained.

Understandability

It may fairly be assumed that information, if it is to be used, must be understood, and that understandability can at least be facilitated by the physical manner in which the material is presented, by the choice of terms or words the report employs, and by the selection of an appropriate combination of different techniques—figures, comments, charts, and graphs.

Many reports—particularly financial reports—are difficult to read and understand. This can, of course, result from the inherent difficulty of the subject matter of the report, or from the fact that the reports are overly complex or poorly constructed, or from a combination of these and other factors. There is a natural and logical basis for wanting reports to be made more understandable, but this can and should be done within practical limits. There is a point at which attempts to simplify should cease, and the businessman should act to increase his capacity for understanding the data the statements contain. The business world today, for example, uses financial statements and financial and other reports so extensively that a businessman is handicapped if he does not understand them and cannot use them. Many businessmen would like to believe that this is not true, but the fact is that financial statements have shown themselves to be so valuable and have enabled so much information to be compressed into so small a space that, rather than being less frequently employed, they are becoming increasingly used as instruments for conveying vital data. Although an executive may not fully understand financial reports initially, he can quickly attain an understanding with a little time and effort, using a textbook on accounting for non-financial executives. The experience of working with the statements themselves and with a financial executive will also teach a lot. It often seems like an onerous chore, but it is usually worthwhile.

This, of course, does not mean that the idea of simplification and the use of appropriate techniques to improve understanding should be abandoned. Just because some statements require or seem to require difficult forms of presentation does not mean that all do or should. As a general rule, overly complex reports conceal rather than reveal, and rows or lists of figures are often hard to understand. Fortunately, a number of devices and techniques can help to reduce the problem. Graphs and charts and verbal explanations can be used to clarify the facts, or devices like colored buttons on display panels or colored tabs on files and similar visual techniques can be used to draw attention to what is in trouble and what is not. Physical units can sometimes be better understood than dollars. "Red flag" reports can concentrate on problems. There are, in short, a great variety of techniques from which to select what is best.

Bases for Comparing Current Results

The final requirement for information is an appropriate basis of comparison. Given everything else—understandable, reliable, timely, and significant data about the present—a basis of comparison is still needed to answer the question: "How am I doing?" The executive needs something to which he can compare the facts. A single number by itself means close to nothing. (If this seems untrue, try to think of a number by itself that does mean something. It is only comparison that gives it meaning.) A fraction reading $\frac{1}{?}$ is interesting as a philosophical springboard, but not as a source of business intelligence. Comparisons are essential. Both the crux of and the answer to the question "How am I doing?" is really to be found in the question: "How am I doing—compared to what?"

There are a number of fundamental comparisons that, taken one by one or together, will bring into focus the essence of the basic question. They, too, can be stated in the form of questions: "How am I doing compared to the present?" "How am I doing compared to the past?" "How am I doing compared to what I planned to do?" "How am I doing compared to what I could do?" "How am I doing compared to my competitors and the industry?" Each of these will be discussed briefly.

1. *The present.* At first glance, it might seem that this

type of comparison is a contradiction in that "How am I doing?" and "the present" are really one and the same. However, there are a number of important comparisons an executive can make that will tell him whether or not the business is in harmony internally. A few examples will illustrate this point. A comparison of current assets to current liabilities will indicate how successful the company will probably be in meeting its current obligations. A comparison of accounts receivable to sales will indicate the number of days of sales which are outstanding. A comparison of unfilled orders to inventory will give at least a rough indication of how well-balanced inventories and customers' demands are. A comparison of shifts worked to shifts available, or of machine down-time to total available time, will give important information about the utilization of facilities. A comparison of net and gross profit to sales will tell how successful the company is in earning more than its costs. All of these and more comparisons of data relating to the same date or to the same period of time can provide an insight into the business that a figure standing by itself cannot hope to provide.

2. *The past.* The past is the second useful basis of comparison, for by comparing present accomplishments with those of prior periods executives can quickly discover in what respects their companies are making progress or falling behind. For example, comparing such matters as present sales with last year's sales or the sales of two years ago, or comparing ratios of inventory turnover with similar ratios in the past, are the forms of comparison most commonly used. In fact, they are about the only comparisons that some companies really make.

This type of comparison has both its weaknesses and its strengths. Past information, to be really comparable, must have the same reliability and accuracy as that pertaining to the present and be recorded and summarized in a way that puts both sets of figures on the same basis. Otherwise, the comparisons will prove inaccurate, with many false signals sent up.

The past, even when accurately, reliably, and comparably recorded, contains inherent weaknesses as a basis of comparison—for reasons that can easily be seen. For example, conditions were different; we were not doing very well at that time—

the Number 3 machine broke down or one of our suppliers was on strike; we were introducing a new product; we had that special order; and so on. Nevertheless, the past has validity or, at least, acceptability because it was what was actually done. It provides a "live" psychological challenge. It measures improvement or regression. As a basis of comparison it does have value.

The past has considerably greater value if a succession of periods is used. A succession of periods establishes a trend, and trends are more important than the results of an individual period. A succession of periods permits comparisons of greater reliability since comparing the present with the trend of the past or with the average of the recent past removes at least some of the unusual or irregular fluctuations from the immediately preceding period. A trend also shows more clearly what is happening. It may be hard to see on the basis of a single month or two that a product is dying, but comparisons extending over a longer period will reveal the facts more clearly.

Finally, the value of the past will depend in part on the selection of an appropriate period with which to make comparisons. Comparisons should not be confined to yearly or to year-to-date periods, for it may be important to be able to compare figures on a monthly, weekly, or even daily basis with similar figures for similar periods in the days, weeks, or months before. The period to be selected should be determined by the significance of the item to current plans, the speed or severity of changes that may develop, and the seasonal behavior pattern of the item involved.

3. *The plan.* The third basis of comparison is to look at the present against a plan. Every year as executives look to the coming year, they make or should make plans to accomplish certain objectives. These objectives and the expenditures to be made in order to accomplish them usually are different from those of the past. Business conditions are different; growth and other objectives have changed; the profit the company expects to achieve differs from year to year.

Comparing actual results with results that are intended and planned can provide some of the most useful information obtainable. Such comparisons will keep the company working to meet its goals; they can tell when and where more vigorous action should be taken to achieve them; they tell when one should consider revising goals and plans; they thus become an integral part of the process of management.

4. *The true potential.* "How am I doing compared to my potential?" is the fourth basis of comparison. This comparison of present and potential—a comparison with what can be done —is made less often in practice than any of the first three bases— current, historical, and planned. Nevertheless, in many ways it is probably as important as any of the others.

Using such a basis of comparison, for example, Lawson could conclude that he was more and more accepting the rate of accomplishment obtained in the past as his goal. Because a finishing machine consistently turns out from 75 to 80 units per hour, the executives have gradually forgotten that its potential rate of production is 100 units per hour. For several years, the manufacturing process has consistently produced scrap or rejected items of about 8 per cent; this has come to be thought of as normal. Is it?

There is a good deal of advantage to adding to other comparisons this comparison of what can be accomplished under close to ideal conditions. If the comparisons with the present, the past, and what was planned to be accomplished are in a sense comparisons with a standard, then comparison with what can be done constitutes a comparison with a more challenging "gold standard." Gold-standard comparisons need not be made as often as some of the others mentioned, for as measures of the potential for improved performance they will change less frequently. With a knowledge of what the potentials are, however, executives can apply both brains and pressure to lift performance nearer to these goals.

5. *The competition.* "How am I doing compared to my competitors?" is the fifth basic comparison available. Most executives appreciate the value of comparing their company's performance with that of their competitors individually or with the industry. The problem usually is not one of interest or desire as much as it is the availability of information with which to make the comparisons. One can, however, give up too easily. There is considerably more information available both about competitors and about the industry than often is realized. For instance, salesmen learn a lot from competitive

dealings in the marketplace or from other business contacts. A great deal of valuable statistical information is available from industry associations. There are industry statistics provided by various credit organizations, banks, government departments, and others. *The Quarterly Financial Report of Manufacturing Corporations* (published by the Federal Trade Commission and the Securities and Exchange Commission), Dun & Bradstreet's *Fourteen Important Ratios,* and Robert Morris Associates' *Statement Studies* are illustrative. Many other data are available besides.

While the information thus obtained may not be as specific as one would like, it is particularly useful in disclosing the more significant events that are taking place and that will take place within the industry. There are limitations imposed by law about the kinds of information that may be collected about sales and sales prices. There are fewer restrictions on the accumulation of information about expenses and costs. Many trade associations collect and report very valuable data to their members about the sales and the operations of a typical company, using industry-wide classifications to help assure that sales and expenses are recorded in a comparable manner by all of the members submitting reports. Many do not pay enough attention to their trade associations and their reports, or they fail to encourage the association to accumulate useful industry-oriented information when it does not.

There are other ways to make competitive comparisons, too. Comparisons can be made between warehouses of the same company where there are two or more essentially similar units to compare. Similar plants can be compared (after making allowances for differences) in a way that will disclose weaknesses and strengths and opportunities for improvement. While, strictly speaking, these are not competitors, they serve some of the same purposes, since the costs and results of two partially independent units can be compared. Access to both units in the comparison serves to simplify obtaining explanations for differences identified for investigation and helps to find out what should be done.

Comparisons can also be made with key aspects of, or even all of, the economy. For example, in selling to the building trade, an excellent measure is found in data about housing

	Present	Past	Plans	Potential	Competitors
			Comparison Can Usually Be Made Usefully With		
Statement of Profit and Loss and Retained Earnings		x	x		x
Balance Sheet		x	x		x
Departmental or Divisional Income and Expense Statements		x	x		
Source and Application of Funds		x	x		
*Cash and Cash Equivalent:					
Ratio to Current Liabilities	x	x	x		x
*Accounts Receivable:					
Ratio to Recent or Average Monthly Credit Sales	x	x	x		?
Ratio of Bad Debts to Credit Sales	x	x	x		
Past-due Accounts—Dollars and Percentages	x	x	x		
*Inventories:					
Dollars—by Classes or Categories		x	x		
Purchase or Manufacturing Costs of Key Items		x	x		
Ratio to Cost of Sales—Total	x	x	x		x
Ratio to Cost of Sales—by Classes or Categories	x	x	x		
Total Current Assets:					
Ratio to Current Liabilities	x	x	x		x
Property, Plant, and Equipment:					
Ratio to Total Assets	x	x	x		x
Ratio to Sales	x	x	x		x
Shareholders' Equity:					
Ratio to Long-Term Debt	x	x	x		x

* See later chapters for other useful kinds of information about these areas.

Fig. 1–1. Bases of comparison for information on current results.

	Present	Past	Plans	Potential	Competitors
				Comparison Can Usually Be Made Usefully With	
Net Profit:					
Ratio to Sales	x	x	x		x
Ratio to Shareholders' Equity (Return on Investment)	x	x	x		x
Ratio to Total Assets	x	x	x		x
Earnings per Share	x	x	x		x
Ratio to Dividends Paid	x	x	x		x
*Sales (Dollars, Quantities, and Unit Prices):					
Total	x	x	x		x
By Product Lines or Other Product Categories	x	x	x		?
By Territories or Other Customer Categories	x	x	x		
Unfilled Orders	x	x	x		
Late Orders	x	x	x		
*Gross Profit:					
Ratio to Sales—Total	x	x	x		x
Ratio to Sales—by Products or Product Line	x	x	x		
Ratio to Sales—by Classes of Customer	x	x	x		
Expenses by Organizational Units and/or Categories:					
Ratio to Sales	x	x	x		
Employees:					
Total and Number by Organizational Unit and Category	x	x	x		
Average Salaries and Wages	x	x	x		
Overtime	x	x	x	x	
*Manufacturing Data:					
Yield	x	x	x	x	
Good Production	x	x	x	x	
Manufacturing Variances by Type	x	x	x	x	
Idle Capacity, Downtime, etc.	x	x	x	x	
Cost per Machine Hour	x	x	x	x	

Fig. 1–1. Continued.

starts. Where a company is a major but competitive supplier of a customer, it can watch the percentage of its customers' sales or costs. Other general or specific economic indicators can often be found. There would seem to be plenty of bases for comparison. Degree of relevance, availability of data, and cost of comparing are three of the major factors to be considered in making a choice.

AN APPROACH TO INFORMATION ON CURRENT RESULTS

"I decided," Lawson's son continued, "to use these criteria in making a first pass at selecting information which we could use to tell us how we stand. The results you can see in this list [Fig. 1–1]. I have tried to choose items which deal with the vital aspects of our business, where I felt that reliable information was or could be made available, and I have tried to find one or more bases for comparison.

"You undoubtedly will wish to study this list, to consider it in terms of your needs, and to suggest those changes you would like to see made."

A knowledge of how one is doing is a matter of crucial importance to Lawson and other business executives with comparable responsibilities. The information needed for this purpose is to some extent similar from company to company and to some extent tailored to fit the individual company's particular requirements. Good information must satisfy certain requirements as to vitality and significance, reliability, availability, understandability, and comparability.

Good information about current progress provides more than inert knowledge—it provides a basis for deciding and for taking action, and acts as a stimulus for managing the company better.

2

Planning and Budgeting

PLANNING AND THE MATURING ENTERPRISE

The second of the key questions every business executive must ask himself is: "Where am I heading?" He must determine not merely where he is heading if he floats with the tide, or even where he is heading if he reacts to those external forces that shape the course of his company's future, but: "Where am I heading if I take steps to decide upon the future I would like to achieve and then move realistically in that direction?"

It is not very difficult to see that a business needs to think about and plan for the future even when the business does not yet exist but is just about to be born. Witness the case of John Carlson, the hypothetical president of a business whose planning problems we shall follow throughout this chapter.

John Carlson, a vice-president of the Greenport Improvement Company, decided one day to go into business for himself. He had nothing but access to money and some ideas about what he wanted to do. "Where am I heading?" "What can I do?" "What should I do?" "What do I want to do?"— these were all questions to be resolved before the character, purpose, and structure of his company could be established. Carlson was probably at the one stage of his career where the need to plan was virtually all-consuming. There were no operations in which to become involved, no results to review and correct—just the need to figure out where he should go. No one needed to tell John Carlson that planning was important at that stage of his career.

After a business begins to operate something seems to happen that leads many business executives to relegate planning

19

to an insignificant role. The pressure of dealing with today leads to the mistaken idea that planning for tomorrow has somehow lost the value which was so clearly evident at the outset of the business. The value of planning—which, in a nutshell, is to make sure that the executive knows "Where am I heading?" and "How am I going to get there?"—has not changed at all. The businessman has two responsibilities—for today and for tomorrow—and while he may have to share his time between them differently, he does have a responsibility for both.

John Carlson, now president of a busy company, began to avoid the question "Where am I heading?" in a rather typical way.

He found himself up to his ears in sales and customers, in manufacturing problems, in handling employees, and in numerous other matters, all clamoring for attention. Planning had become something done on the fly or to be done next month. Actually, deep down, he had come to feel that planning was not too important any more, since what he hoped and expected to do was pretty well established by what had happened in the past—by the kind of services he rendered, by the kind of plant and facilities he owned, by his own capabilities and those of his employees, and by the nature of developments in the area he served. Carlson felt that by mentally adjusting past results he, in essence, had his plan and that nothing more would be needed.

WHAT PLANNING REALLY MEANS

Planning is, of course, the term used to describe the process of determining "Where am I heading?" It is the process by which, after a consideration of the significant internal and external factors of the past, present, and future, the businessman can see more clearly and realistically where it is he wants to and can go. He then can select a course of action with greater assurance that it will be correct than would be possible if he relied upon a more dimly seen view developed more or less intuitively as a by-product of making day-to-day decisions. Some would say that planning is the process of making things happen that would not be likely to happen as quickly, as often, or as well if they relied solely on the cumulative impact of day-to-day decisions to achieve the desired result.

As an example, it is easy to see that those who manage the nation's space program are more apt to achieve their objectives if they realistically establish goals and then determine how to use their resources to accomplish these complex ends. The necessity of proceeding in this manner—quite clear in the case of the space program because of its innovative character and its scope—may not be so apparent, however, even on a proportionate scale in the case of managing a more normal type of business. Yet, if a businessman does not decide what he wants to do in advance, the chances that he will actually accomplish what he later may decide he actually wanted to do are pretty slim. If an executive decides he would like to accomplish certain goals and then does not organize his resources for this purpose, the chances of success also will be reduced. Planning, in fact, is essential in every kind of enterprise.

"On-the-Fly" Planning Is Not Enough

Quite obviously, a president who arrives at the conclusion that mentally adjusting past results is enough will have done so honestly, for more than anyone else he is interested in the success of his company. He will probably, however, be making a mistake. Why? Because he does not adequately realize (1) the variety or power of the forces potentially affecting his company, (2) his own ability to influence the future in his favor, or (3) the difficulty of figuring out the net impact of various factors and forces on "where he was heading" without giving it some time and thought. Let us look once more at Carlson.

Carlson felt that by mentally adjusting past results he, in essence, had a plan. In a way, he had a point—but only if he had a company with a secure niche in the business world, a love of the status quo, and, among other things:

No reason to grow.
No changes in labor rates or material prices ahead.
No new products of any significance to introduce.
No major old products whose sales were declining.
No important changes in sales prices.

No important changes in the quality or volume of requirements of customers.

No significant differences in his competitors' actions.

The possibility that Carlson actually had such a static situation was remote, for few businesses exist in such a state of isolation.

FORCES AFFECTING THE FUTURE

The purpose of planning, it might be well to repeat, is to predict in an orderly fashion the influences to which a company should respond, and to set in motion those forces and actions that will result in more favorable results than would otherwise occur. What are some of these factors and forces? A few are listed below.

1. External—largely beyond the individual company's control
    Development of new or improved competitive products with an advantage in cost, quality, or availability.
    Changes in the volume or type of business of present or potential customers, which in turn affect the supplier's volume of sales or alter the specifications of the products required from him.
    Additional competitors furnishing the same goods or services.
    Changes in credit policies.
    Improvements in materials or parts available from competitive suppliers.
    Improvements in machinery and equipment.
    Development of new packaging and transportation methods.
    Changes in economic conditions for the industry or business as a whole.
2. Internal—established by the characteristics of the company as it now exists
    Financial resources.
    Capabilities of managerial, technical, and other staffs and employees.
    Capabilities of present machinery and equipment.
    Size and location of plant.
    Costs of producing goods and services.
3. Entrepreneurial—reflecting the desires of the owner and management

Desire to diversify or to shift dependence from a product with uncertain demand.

Desire to grow in order to produce greater profits, more opportunities for employees, and so forth.

Desire to raise the quality of products and services.

Desire to move into additional geographical markets.

Desire to increase profitability of money invested.

Evidently, if many of these factors or additional unlisted forces are involved, a plan will be helpful in establishing what can and should be done in the future. Let us look again at the forces acting on Carlson and his business.

Carlson's company was not immune to internal and external forces nor to his own entrepreneurial desires as its owner-president. Among them were:

His new labor contract increased costs by 3 percent.

His largest customer's quality requirements went up; to meet them meant a 5 percent increase in labor on that product, together with a new machine costing $100,000.

Carlson developed a new product which he believed would add 40 percent to his sales within three years, but it needed to be delivered quickly "off the shelf" and required that he either buy $150,000 of equipment or go into a third shift.

Carlson decided to set up two sales branches and warehouses in communities about 100 miles away to expand his territory and reduce his dependence on a very small geographical area. He began to worry that he would run out of cash.

It occurred to him that other things might be about to happen to the company about which he knew little or nothing, and that there might be other things he would like to make happen by putting some effort into them.

Carlson began to realize that certain restrictions upon where he would like to be heading were already imposed by the facts of what he was now. He realized that he had certain assets and liabilities, certain products and costs, certain customers, certain facilities, certain sources of funds, certain opportunities, and other significant constraints. Carlson discovered that his company had certain characteristics that served to limit his freedom of choice. As he thought about them, however, he realized that while they limited him in some respects, they were far from being so restrictive that he could not select what he wanted to do from a wide range of alternatives.

HOW PLANNING IS DONE

What are Carlson's, or any other president's, alternatives, and how should he go about planning for them?

Determining "Where am I heading?" requires adequate information, adequate executive participation, and adequate time. Without all of these, the plan will be more form than substance, and, if used as a course of action, may well do more harm than good. Adequate information is needed so that the plan may be based as nearly as is practicable on "the facts."

Adequate executive participation is needed because the key executives alone, particularly in small businesses, are in a position to evaluate the external and internal factors mentioned above and to set the company's entrepreneurial goals. Adequate time is needed because the plan is important and not self-evident. Uninterrupted time is necessary because thinking the program through requires that a number of interrelated, often complex decisions be made. Let us see how this was undertaken in Carlson's case.

After Carlson decided that he had more to wrestle with than he had originally thought, he decided to do it right. He determined to start running the business before it started running him. He decided to get together his figures and consult with a couple of his key executives. He set aside specific hours, when they would not be interrupted, to work on developing their plans. They took data largely provided by the answers to "How am I doing?" They studied the trends of sales and the profitability of various product lines and products; they thought about and discussed with customers and others (even competitors) future trends in sales and prices and the probable inroads of competitive products. They discussed their customers' needs for tighter specifications and higher quality. They looked at some of the data published by their industry and others. They talked with their banker and their accountant. They talked about what they would like to do and what they could practically do. They thought of the implications of their tentative plans in terms of equipment needs; of the manpower requirements on the executive, technical, and lower levels; of the availability of cash or loans; of the increase in receivables and inventories; and so on. Then they sat down and worked out a plan—not just once but often, to find the proper fit of objectives, profits, and resources. They made projections of the balance sheet, the P&L statement, and the inflow and outflow of cash. They talked of how the banks would react to a request for additional loans, and of corporate dividend policies. And, finally, they created a plan—or, rather, two plans. One rather explicit plan covered the current year (the budget). The other, more general, covered the next three years (the "long-range" plan). Each plan was expressed in numbers so that it could be clearly understood. Each was expressed largely in dollars so that the different elements could be interrelated and the financial impact determined. As far as possible, the plans followed the same format as the regular monthly reports so that it would be possible to tell what progress was being made and whether the initial plan was wrong and should be modified, stretched out, or substantially changed. The responsibility for some identifiable part of each plan was assigned to one of the key executives. When such assignments were clearly not for a subordinate, the president took on the responsibility himself.

What Carlson did is not much different from what any other company can profitably do. He faced the questions other business executives face and took the steps they can take to plan successfully. He projected the effects that important influences would have on his company and determined how best to respond to them. He took the initiative, too, and decided not only how he would respond but also how he would create influences to work in his favor. This is exactly what the businessman can and should do for his company—produce a blueprint of the future in the form of operating, capital, and cash budgets which depict what he wants his company to be in terms of what he realistically believes it can accomplish. The process is shown pictorially in Fig. 2–1.

Planning Is a Continuing Process

One of the more interesting and disquieting things about plans is that they rarely work out quite as anticipated. As any experienced planner will quickly say, the future has uncertainties, and any plan, especially one that involves a significant

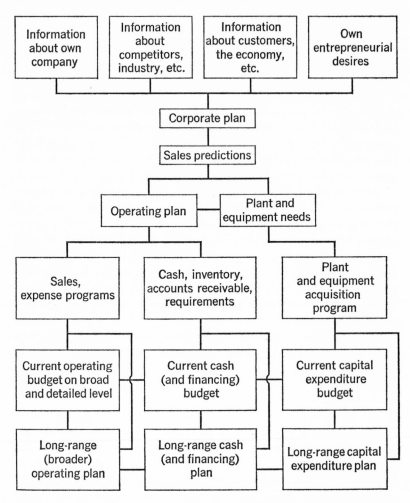

Fig. 2–1. Corporate planning—a flow chart.

change in the nature of a business, may not be realized in full. Uncertainties can be minimized to a degree by good information or by extra efforts or resources, but they can never be entirely removed. A plan may turn out wrong because the assumptions on which it was based were not completely accurate. The future may be different because the company is unable to achieve its goals at the speed or to the degree it felt possible, using its present and future resources. A plan may turn out to be incorrect because at the same time that one business executive is planning his moves, another businessman in another company will be planning to make moves of which the first is unaware.

Planning is a continuing process. Plans must be remade as well as made. A periodic reconsideration is obviously necessary in order to see whether (1) the assumptions on which the plans have been made need to be revised; (2) the company's rate of progress needs or permits a change; and (3) the basic goals and objectives of the plan need to be altered.

This reconsideration, or "budget review" as it is sometimes called, should be scheduled on a regular basis to make sure that it is done and done adequately. Fortunately, except when major decisions are involved, the process of review and revision should consume a relatively small amount of executive time. The need for regular review is illustrated by what happened to Carlson six months after he completed his plans.

After one particularly perturbing day, Carlson realized that the product that he had hoped would add 40 per cent to his company's sales still contained some design defects. He was certain that these could be overcome and that the product would ultimately be as successful as he had hoped. It appeared to him, however, that a delay of some six months would probably be involved.

On the other hand, Carlson had found that his experiment in setting up two sales branches and warehouses in communities about 100 miles away was so successful that he selected two more communities and decided to proceed in the same manner there. Carlson also noted, when he compared the monthly reports designed to indicate "how he was doing" with his plans, that certain other assumptions were not quite valid and that in some respects the company was not moving toward its objectives as well or as rapidly as he had hoped.

Carlson and the other executives who had helped him with the original plan decided to meet again to talk things over. They followed substantially the same procedure that had proved successful in developing the initial plan. This time, however, they were able to restrict most of their attention to the changes they wished to make or felt they had to make to respond to the present conditions. They adjusted the operating, cash, and capital expenditure budgets. They found that not only was there a change in their predictions of their total operating results, but also a change in the periods in which they would be required to have cash available for the capital and other expenditures required to get the new branches and the new products going. The revised plan did not take very long to prepare. It gave all three executives a common understanding of what the revised program was to be and helped to assure them that the right actions would be taken at the right time and in the proper sequence. Thus, the planning process was continued and insured the continued control of the destiny of the business.

Dealing with Complications

The smaller the number and the impact of the forces affecting a company's future, the simpler, of course, is the work involved in preparing a plan. The simplicity or complexity of a plan thus will vary with the nature of the company and the industry, as well as with the company's own state of development. In some periods or in some companies, capital expenditure planning will be extremely important. In others, sales and product planning will loom larger, or the manner in which research and development money will be spent will be significant, or manpower planning will be extensively involved.

It can be generally said that planning tends to become more complex when one or a combination of the following three frequently occurring situations exists:

1. Major capital expenditures are involved.
2. Major new products are to be introduced.
3. The outcome of a set of actions is very uncertain.

1. *Planning capital expenditures.* Planning is complicated when major capital expenditures are involved. First, there is the problem of deciding which of a variety of proposed expenditures should be made. If the item to be acquired by the capital expenditure is expected to last over a period of years, there must be an estimate of its ability to save money, increase sales, and otherwise increase profits over its life. This means that planning must, to the extent that it affects the profitability

of the proposed investment, extend in at least a general way over the life of the investment. If the equipment is useful for a variety of purposes, the problem is not too great; if the equipment is specialized—particularly if it is pretty well restricted to single groups of products—the problem is much more difficult.

Capital expenditures planning also involves planning for cash, unless the property acquired is to be leased. The reason for this is obvious: the expenditure is immediate while the return from both depreciation and profits is delayed. Thus, capital expenditures planning must be related to the cash budget—to the total flow of cash from internal sources and from funds supplied by shareholders, long-term lenders, and banks.

2. *Planning new products.* Planning ahead for the introduction of a major new product is also complex. Estimates of profitability and of the funds required for equipment, inventories, receivables, and so on, are required, along with a determination of the period in which they will be needed. The outgo, once again, precedes the receipt of cash. Cash budgeting, part of the subject of Chapter 6, is an integral part of new product planning.

3. *Planning under conditions of uncertainty.* A third kind of complexity exists when the outcome of a set of actions that the company "plans" to take is very uncertain, or where the conditions that will exist are difficult to predict. In these cases, two courses are open to the president. He can make provision for a continuing review and revision of plans on a monthly, quarterly (the usual), or annual basis as circumstances may require; or he can make alternate plans at the outset so that he can "fall back" from the plan he is following to a "prepared position."

The first of the alternatives is merely the normal planning procedure, carried out more frequently or intensively. The second is the more drastic and is usually undertaken when ordinary replanning procedures would be too slow.

CENTRAL ROLE OF INFORMATION

Where does information fit into all of this? (1) The plan or budget itself is information, usually in numbers, which becomes not only an important device for directing the efforts of management but, in turn, a part of the information system of the future. (2) Plans and budgets rely on other information available in records and reports within and without the company for most of the information about the past and a fair share of the basis for predicting what will happen in the future.

Plans and budgets are not merely a lot of numbers, prepared so that the businessman can have a new kind of report. They are prepared to be a guide to, and a measure of, management's future actions. Formal plans and budgets do not necessarily take a lot of time to prepare. It is the quality of the thought producing these relatively few numbers that counts.

"Where am I heading?"—a most significant question for the businessman—can be seen as another way of saying "Do I have a plan?" Do I have a plan (produced as the result of adequate information, time, and executive participation) that will result in defining where I want my company to go in terms of external forces, the internal resources of the company, and my own or the owners' desires as businessmen? Having defined the company's future in such terms, do I have a plan that shows how the company's present and future resources will be used to bring this about?

The business executive answering the question "Where am I heading?" in the manner outlined in this book will obviously acquire a plan. More than that, he will have acquired the habit of planning. He will discover that what he originally thought of as fruitless or time-wasting work which interfered with getting things done actually sharpened the focus of his efforts to a point where he began to accomplish more. He will see how his preoccupation with the "day-to-day" was often a stumbling block for himself and his associates and that tomorrow became today more quickly than he had supposed.

3

Costs, Prices, and Profits

A DECLINING-PROFIT PROBLEM

Harris Manufacturing Company had been in the business of making and selling fans for many years. It had developed a product line with a variety of models, which it sold through various channels to wholesalers and retailers, and even directly to contractors and industrial customers. The company had many strengths but one obvious and serious problem: while its sales were growing, its profits were not. At a meeting with his key executives, the president, Richard Harris, noted his dissatisfaction and concern over the company's poor profit performance and expressed his determination to bring about an improvement as rapidly as possible.

As he said, "I've been looking at our profit picture for the last four years and about all I can conclude is that we must be establishing something of a record for futility—running harder and having less to show for it. If I take the controller's figures, this is what they show:

	Sales	Net Profit	Percentage on Sales
19x1	$3,600M	$280M	7.8%
19x2	4,000	300	7.5
19x3	4,200	250	6.0
19x4	4,500	200	4.4

"Not only are we selling more and making less on a percentage basis, but, worse yet, our actual total dollars of profit have declined. We've got to do something; I guess that's obvious to all of us."

Two points of view were set forth as to how this should be done. One of the executives stated that the way to bring about an improvement in profits was for each executive, both personally and through his assistants, to try as hard as possible to increase sales, to increase selling prices, and to decrease manufacturing, selling, administrative, and other costs. He asserted his belief that the only thing that would improve conditions was action and expressed the opinion that most of those present had at least some idea of what the problems were.

Breaking Down the Problem

The controller both agreed and disagreed. "We can all agree that, in the long run, only action brings results. I think much of what is proposed is sound as far as it goes, and that we should increase our efforts in areas where we know we should take action right away. However, I also think we do not know enough about our business to know where our weak spots are.

"We think we have a simple business, and in a way we do; but we also have our complications. We don't have one business; we have three businesses and maybe several subdivisions besides. Our company really looks like this:

"1. We sell the Harris line of fans. They vary considerably in price, cost, quality, and physical characteristics, but essentially they fall in the moderate-to-high price range. These fans, as you know, are ultimately purchased primarily for home use from department stores, discount houses, hardware stores, appliance stores, and similar retail outlets with which the general public usually deals. We promote these fans as Harris fans and support their sale with a fair amount of cooperative advertising and point-of-sale display. Most of our sales are made through the efforts of our own sales force, with a sprinkling of sales by commission agents in regions where our sales are small.

"2. We make a lot of fans to Kellogg's specifications, which the Kellogg Department Store chain sells under its own name. Most of these fans are in the low-to-medium price range. We provide no sales support, and essentially our problem is to deliver fans that meet their specifications, on time, to the relatively few places where their stores are located. Our sales vice-president handles this account himself but, except for the annual negotiation period, which takes a short but intensive burst of his efforts, there isn't too much involved so long as we meet their quality requirements and delivery schedule.

"3. We have a line of industrial fans intended to be used to meet specific industrial requirements for ventilation. Most of these are either replacements ordered by industrial customers or original equipment specified by engineers or contractors. We don't so much sell these fans as we do our ability to make them when they are needed, and so our sales force, our technical and sales support, and our technical literature are quite different. As you know, this is a fairly new venture, and our modest sales are still far from what we hope they ultimately will be.

"With such a mixture of manufacturing specifications and costs, order sizes, selling expenses, advertising costs, and selling prices, we would be hard put to say where we are making or losing money, and how much. I guess it's my fault for not having produced this information in the past or at least for not having it all at my fingertips—but I didn't and I don't and that's that.

"It seems to me, though, that if we know where our problems are, we can more effectively direct our efforts toward solving them. Then our actions will be more effective, because we will have identified the areas in which our efforts are needed and in which opportunities for action exist.

"What I'd like to suggest is that you begin to take action on the things you believe need to be done. In the meantime, I will analyze some of the data I have available to me, and try to pinpoint some of the major problems. I'll have to make some assumptions and allocate some costs, but I feel I can produce something useful rather quickly."

The problem that faced Harris and his associates is a common one. It is encountered in most companies, whether they are selling products that they manufacture or merchandise that they purchase, or rendering services. No matter what their level of total profit, there will almost surely be certain products, services, customers, and/or distribution channels that produce more or less in sales, costs, expenses, and profits (or losses) than do the others.

This chapter will attempt to show how better information about costs, prices, and profits can help to improve profits and how a balanced approach—with intelligent action being taken on the basis of sound information—can produce, as it does in so many other aspects of business management, good results. It will also show the role of the special analysis in contrast to as well as in conjunction with the regular report.

SPECIAL COST AND PROFIT ANALYSES

The controller had been producing a set of reports setting forth quite acceptably the status of the company as a whole. He had produced the following information:

Balance sheet.
Profit and loss and retained earnings.
Sales by products.
Manufacturing costs.
Selling expenses.
General and administrative expenses.

In all except the balance sheet he showed both budgeted and actual results. These statements were, in fact, the source of the data that Harris had cited. The information thus conveyed was correct, and it quite properly showed that there was a problem. The information was not, however, sufficiently detailed to pinpoint the problem and to suggest the area in which action was needed.

It was this that the controller proceeded to remedy by means of special analyses. He took figures directly from the books or made analyses of the records that had been summarized for entry into them. He summarized sales, expenses, and costs into different and more detailed classifications—at times making allocations on what he felt to be logical bases, at times assigning income and expenses directly.

Analyzing the Company by Line of Business

The controller decided that the most important thing to do was to break apart total sales, costs, and expenses to show how well the company was doing in its three major lines—

Harris, Kellogg, and industrial. His analysis was made in the following manner:

Sales were analyzed by retabulating sales invoices into the three-way breakdown shown in Fig. 3–1.

Cost of sales was reallocated, using information on unit costs that had been developed by the company's cost system.

Each category of selling and administrative expenses was reviewed and assigned to the three product lines on an estimated basis— sometimes by percentage of effort and sometimes by percentage of value received.

As a result, the analysis shown in Fig. 3–1 was prepared.

	Company as a Whole	Harris Line	Kellogg Line	Industrial
Sales	$4,500M	$2,700M	$1,100M	$ 700M
Cost of Sales	2,700	1,300	900	500
Gross Profit .	1,800	1,400	200	200
Selling and Distribution Expenses . .	900	600	100	200
General and Administrative Expenses	500	350	100	50
	1,400	950	200	250
Profit or (Loss) Before Income Taxes	400	450	–	(50)
Provision for Income Taxes	200	225		(25)
Net Profit or (Loss) .	$ 200M	$ 225M	$ – M	$(25)M
Units Sold		90,000	90,000	8,000

Fig. 3–1. Analysis of profit by line of business (conventional method); Schedule 1.

A similar analysis for the two preceding years indicated that the situation was roughly the same for those years and that, while sales were growing in each line of business, less attractive results were being achieved in the first two categories while the third was just about holding its own.

The controller reported his findings to the president. "The analysis I have made," he said, "can be challenged—particularly the allocation of certain costs and expenses that can't be directly associated with a particular line of products—but it's as fair an analysis as I know how to make. I'm certainly not trying to prove any preconceived notions I might have had; as a matter of fact, I was sort of surprised at the results. I'm willing to stand behind the report as being a pretty close indication of how we are doing, where we are, and the fact that we are not making money."

Analyzing the Company by Variability of Costs

Harris looked at the figures for a while. "They seem to confirm what I expected, I'm afraid. However, I can't see how they tell me what to do. We may be spinning our wheels on the Kellogg line, but I can't see giving up 90,000 units and having all that capacity sitting idle; and for sentimental reasons, if nothing else, I can't see that we should scuttle the industrial business—not with its potential. I tell you what you do, though: figure out how we'd be if we didn't have the Kellogg business and how many more Harris fans we'd have to sell to stay even."

To make this analysis, the controller had to introduce several new ideas about costs and their behavior. He had to recognize that (1) all costs do not vary directly with volume, (2) the level of those that do not vary with volume can be established by long-term actions (such as the existence of a plant) or by shorter-term actions (such as the overhead costs needed to provide a capability of producing 150,000, 200,000, or 250,000 units a year), or can be deliberately set by management at a given level (as in the case of research programs or advertising programs). Giving recognition to these concepts, the controller produced the analysis in Fig. 3–2.

This analysis indicated that (1) cost and expense patterns varied substantially among the three product lines, and (2) the company had a fairly heavy commitment to maintaining a good volume of business. Obviously, the controller had to make some judgments about how quickly changes could be

	Company as a Whole	Harris Line	Kellogg Line	Industrial
Sales	$4,500M	$2,700M	$1,100M	$ 700M
Variable Costs:				
Manufacturing	2,100	1,000	700	400
Selling and Distribution	350	250	50	50
Total Variable Costs	2,450	1,250	750	450
Marginal Income	2,050	1,450	350	250
Committed and Programmed Costs:				
Programmed Costs	400	300	20	80
Committed Costs:				
Can Be Changed Substantially in 6 Months to 1 Yr.	700	400	150	150
Can Be Changed Only Over a Longer Period	550	300	180	70
Total Committed and Programmed Costs	1,650	1,000	350	300
Profit or (Loss) Before Income Taxes	400	450	—	(50)
Provision for Income Taxes	200	225	—	(25)
Net Profit or (Loss)	$ 200M	$ 225M	$ —	$(25)M
Units Sold		90,000	90,000	8,000

Fig. 3–2. Analysis of profit by line of business (variable, committed, and programmed costs); Schedule 2.

made, if the decision was to alter the volume of business in a major way. He accomplished this with the help of executives in the manufacturing, sales, and other key departments.

The controller then undertook to use the data he had developed to project what he thought might happen. He examined the way in which Harris line costs varied as volume changed, and made a budget for each volume level from 60,000 to 130,000 units in intervals of 10,000 units. The committed costs were rather fixed in nature and varied slowly as the volume changed. The programmed costs, he and the president decided, were sure to increase as they passed 120,000 units, primarily because greater advertising would be needed to reach new markets and cultivate old ones more intensively. Variable costs he projected as changing in direct proportion to the number of units produced.

Profit Variances with Volume

The controller then had to decide what to do with the costs remaining after giving up the Kellogg volume. After discussion with Harris, he decided to consider that only the "long-term committed costs" would remain after a year or so had gone by, and prepared the analysis on that basis.

The analysis shown in Fig. 3–3 resulted.

At that point, the controller decided he could present his findings in a more readily understandable form if he also prepared a chart (Fig. 3–4)—commonly called a break-even chart —showing pictorially what Fig. 3–3 indicated.

Analyzing Gross Profit by Products

While the controller was working on this analysis he asked his cost clerk to put together some information as to costs, selling prices, and volumes for specific products in both the Harris and the Kellogg lines, wherever possible putting comparable items opposite each other on the schedule. This produced the results shown in Fig. 3–5.

USING COST AND PROFIT ANALYSES

The controller knew there was other information he might find useful, but he decided there was enough in the reports he had already prepared for a productive discussion of the company's problems. Before the meeting took place he sent all five schedules (Figs. 3–1 through 3–5) to the other executives. Certain explanatory comments accompanied the schedules, but no attempt was made to reach conclusions as to what the data meant or to make recommendations on what should be done.

Harris started out the meeting: "I am amazed at what these numbers show and at how well I can understand what they seem to mean, even with my limited knowledge of financial affairs. I can also see how we could argue about whether they are exactly right. I think that such arguments will just get us

Units	60M	70M	80M	90M	100M	110M	120M	130M
Long-Term Committed Costs	$290M	$290M	$300M	$300M	$300M	$310M	$310M	$320M
Short-Term Committed Costs	370	380	390	400	410	420	430	440
Programmed Costs	250	300	300	300	300	300	350	400
Total	910	970	990	1,000	1,010	1,030	1,090	1,160
Variable Costs	875	1,000	1,125	1,250	1,375	1,500	1,625	1,750
Total Costs	1,785	1,970	2,115	2,250	2,385	2,530	2,715	2,910
Sales	1,800	2,100	2,400	2,700	3,000	3,300	3,600	3,900
Pre-Tax Profit	15	130	285	450	615	770	885	990
Long-Term Loss (from unused Kellogg facilities and inability to share certain programmed research)	240	240	240	240	240	230	230	220
Net Pre-Tax Profit or (Loss)	$(225)M	($110)M	$45M	$210M	$375M	$540M	$655M	$770M

Fig. 3–3. Profit predictions at various volume levels; Schedule 3 (Harris line).

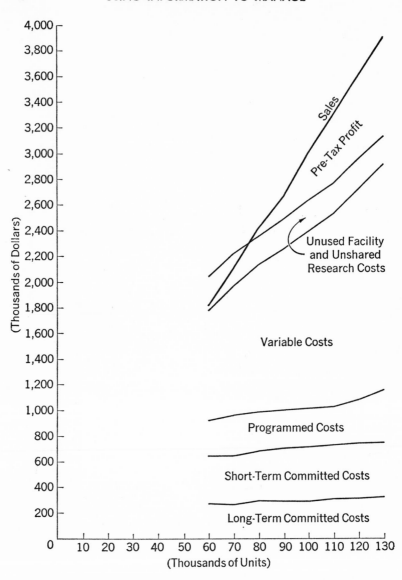

Fig. 3–4. Profit predictions at various volume levels; Schedule 4 (Harris line).

Harris Line

Model No.	Average Sales Price	Average Cost	"Card" Cost *	Average Gross Profit
H 601	$50	$22	$23	$28
H 601A	52	25	24	27
H 601D	52	25	24	27
H 752	43	18	19	25
H 810	40	19	20	21
H 810A	42	22	21	20
H 810D	42	22	21	20
H 901	30	14	14	16
H 901H	30	21	16	9
H 905A	20	12	12	8
H 905D	23	15	13	8
H 905G	25	15	15	10
H 999	15	12	9	3

Kellogg Line

Model No.	Average Sales Price	Average Cost	"Card" Cost *	Average Gross Profit
K 1000A	$24	$20	$18	$4
K 1008	24	20	18	4
K 1025A	13	11	11	2
K 1025D	16	13	13	3
K 1100A	14	12	12	2
K 1100B	12	10	10	2
K 1200	10	9	8	1
K 1500	8	7	6	1

* A term used at Harris Manufacturing to indicate what the product *should* cost per the plant's estimate.

Fig. 3–5. Gross profit on certain models; Schedule 5.

off the track, and therefore I suggest that unless something develops to make us believe the numbers are wrong, we assume they are accurate enough for our purposes.

"Schedule 1 [Fig. 3–1], as I see it, shows that the only place we make money is on the Harris line, that we break even on Kellogg, and that we lose a bit on the industrial business. We aren't going to touch the industrial business for a variety of reasons, we all agree. I asked our controller, therefore, to get together some figures on the Harris and Kellogg lines that he thought might help us. This he seems to have done very well. Perhaps it would be well if he explained them to us."

Variable, Committed, and Programmed Costs

"Schedule 2 [Fig. 3–2]," the controller began, "takes the same overall information that is shown in Schedule 1, but presents it in another form, showing roughly how the costs and profits vary in relation to our ability to control them and change them. The variable costs of manufacturing, selling, and distribution are determined almost directly by the number of units we make and sell. These costs represent direct labor, direct materials, some kinds of manufacturing overhead, sales commissions, point-of-sale advertising displays, and so on. The data show that, on an average unit for the two lines, we make a marginal income of $16.10 on Harris and $3.89 on Kellogg:

	Harris	Kellogg
Sales	$30.00	$12.22
Variable Costs	13.90	8.33
Marginal Income	$16.10	$ 3.89

"This means that, within reasonable changes of volume, every additional unit we sell makes us $16.10 and $3.89, respectively (or that we lose the opportunity to make it, if we don't sell it).

"There is a whale of a difference between the marginal income we make and our net income. As you can see, the marginal income has to cover all of our other costs before we really make anything. These other costs I have called programmed and committed costs to show how we can change them, and within what limits over how long a period of time.

"Programmed costs—sometimes called 'managed costs'—are

the result of programs we as management decide to undertake. In these programs there is a considerable amount of latitude as to how much we spend and when. Generally, however, once we decide to spend the money, our expenditures for programmed costs are not going to change very much whether our volume of business goes up or down, unless or until we decide to do something about them. The two main items in the figure of $400,000 are our general advertising program and the rather limited amount of new product research that we do.

"The committed costs are something else again. These are the costs we incur by being in business—they are required to produce and sell our fans. We can change some of them fairly rapidly once we decide to make a big change in our volume of business, but some we can change only with great difficulty unless we just plain go out of business. In the shorter-term category are most of our supervisors, most of the people in departments like personnel—or accounting, for that matter. Long-term committed costs include depreciation, insurance, real estate taxes, the president's salary, and other costs you can think of. Some people call committed costs 'capacity costs' or the 'costs of being ready to do business.'

"You can see that the programmed and committed costs are quite high for Harris and a good deal lower for Kellogg—especially on a per-unit basis. Since they do not vary very much in total—at least with small changes in volume—the unit cost changes rapidly. You can see this from Schedule 3 [Fig. 3–3], where I figured the Harris line cost levels at various production volumes. There the unit cost of programmed and committed costs varies from $15.17 at 60,000 units to $11.11 for 90,000 units to $9.08 for 120,000.

"So much for theory. What does Schedule 2 actually say? It says the same thing about our net profits as Schedule 1, but it also says that every additional unit of Harris sold should be worth $16.10 to the company instead of the $3.89 we would make if it were a Kellogg fan. The second thing it indicates, of course, is that if we sold 180,000 Harris fans on the same basis as we now do, we would make twice as much money as we presently do with our 90,000–90,000 split.

"A third thing which might seem to be indicated, but is not, is that we would be just as well off if we dropped the Kellogg

line since all we do is break even on it anyway. The problem
—and I'm sure you don't need any figures to demonstrate it—
is that we'd have to pay for a lot of unused capacity, we couldn't
share some of our research expense, and we'd really have to
tear our company apart to bring it down to about 60 per cent
of its present size."

Profit Predictions Under Varying Conditions

"In spite of the fact that I don't think we should do it," the
controller continued, "I did make up Schedule 2 to show what
would happen if we dropped the Kellogg line and succeeded,
after a year or so, in eliminating all our short-term committed
costs. This schedule and the break-even chart in Schedule 4
[Fig. 3–4] show us that we still would make some money even
if our Harris sales remained at 90,000 units, and that we would
just about do what we do now at somewhere near 105,000
units—a sales increase of a bit more than 15 per cent. Obviously, one of the major things to be decided is what to do
about the Kellogg business.

"Before you think about that, however, you might want to
look at Schedule 5 [Fig. 3–5], the last schedule I prepared.
This schedule shows the average sales price, actual and 'card'
costs, and gross profit based on our actual costs for our major
products. Where we have a model which compares quite
closely with one of Kellogg's, I have listed them on the same
line; where there is a blank in one column or the other, it
means there is no comparable item."

The controller's explanation produced the following discussion.

PRESIDENT: "I can see from the break-even chart you have
shown us [Fig. 3–4] that our profit rises sharply as we increase
sales of Harris fans. Would the same thing happen if Kellogg
sales were increased?"

CONTROLLER: "The answer is no. The profits would increase,
of course, but at a rate of less than $4.00 for every unit instead
of the $16.00 per unit we can expect from Harris. Stated in
another way, 10,000 additional Kellogg units would produce
on the average a profit before taxes of about $40,000. The rea-

son for this, of course, is that our sales price for Kellogg is much lower and our ratio of variable to total costs is much higher for the Kellogg line than for Harris. We just don't have much leverage."

MARKETING V.P.: "As I see it, the same thing is not true if we can increase the sales price to Kellogg or reduce our costs. Costs aren't my business, but sales prices are. The Kellogg men are tough negotiators all right, but they need us as much as we need them. They certainly can't expect us to work for nothing: we take risks; we work hard; we use our skills; we are certainly entitled to a reasonable return on what we have invested in the business. With these and any other figures you think would be helpful, I'm willing to tackle them for about 5 per cent more. If we could manage that, it would increase our sales about 60 cents a unit or about $55,000 overall—all of which would go straight down to net (or at least net before taxes). If you could get another 5 per cent out of costs, this would be quite a bit more respectable. What do you think— can that be done?"

MANUFACTURING V.P.: "We can try, but as you know we have pounded pretty hard on that line for quite a while. I do see, though, looking at the last schedule, that we are running over our 'card' costs on both our highest-cost and our lowest-cost models. I have a sneaking suspicion that the reasons for this may be just exactly the opposite and that what we do about it should therefore be quite different. The K1000 models, which are the most expensive, are costing us more than they should because (1) our runs are shorter than they might be, and (2) we have some production inefficiencies that we still have to eliminate. I don't need to discuss the first problem now; the second, I think we should be able to take care of with a bit more effort and some changes we can make in production techniques. The low-priced models—the 1200 and 1500 —are something else again. In my opinion, our 'card' costs must be wrong. You will recall that Kellogg pushed us very hard for a low-priced fan, and we sharpened our pencils very fine to try to give it to them. I think we just talked ourselves into thinking that our 'card costs' were $8.00 and $6.00; I don't believe they are at all. $9.00 and $7.00 may not be exactly right but they are closer. When we talk with Kellogg, I suggest that we really push hard on these two models; it's not our costs but our selling prices that are wrong here."

PRESIDENT: "When I look at Schedule 5 [Fig. 3–5], I get some other ideas that we should look into, too. First, we have some obvious weak spots in the Harris line. Why should we make less on the A and D versions than on the plain? We started these to make more—not less—of a margin. Second, what's the matter with our 900 series, especially with 901 and 999? Third, if the Kellogg series and the Harris line are that much alike, can't we make them even more alike, so we can save on design costs, lower purchase prices on larger quantities, longer runs, and so on? Fourth, can't we interest Kellogg in upgrading its line of fans with some of the more expensive models, on which we make a higher return per fan? Finally, should we begin to pay higher rates of commission for selling the fans on which we make real money and less on the low-profit items, instead of a straight percentage of sales?

"When I look at Schedule 3 [Fig. 3–3] and see how our profits go up with an increase in the volume of Harris fans, I wonder if we're putting enough effort into selling them. Today isn't the day to talk about it, but I believe we should consider whether we should spend more on promotion, whether we should try to extend our geographical area a bit more even if we can't recover all the freight, and any other ideas we can develop that would increase our sales at a reasonable increase in expense.

"I'm impressed by how much we have in these so-called committed costs. They represent quite a lot to handle. When we get a little further along I'd like us to look at them—what they are, which of us is responsible for them, how we decide how much of them we are going to have, and, quite honestly, what we have now that we can do without—or at least how we can make them vary more rapidly with our profits and our volume of production than they do at present.

"I think it's quite clear that much of the information the controller prepared for us has been very helpful. I don't know whether to thank him for it or to bawl him out for not producing it before. I do know we need something like this in the future—maybe not all of it, or all of it all the time, but we obviously do need to have a better knowledge of what's going on in the business than we have had in the past. I consider it the controller's responsibility to see that we have it. He has the records and knows what can be drawn out of them."

REPORTS MOST FREQUENTLY FOUND USEFUL

The information that best suits the needs of Harris Manufacturing Company reflects both the kind of business in which the company is engaged and the situation in which it finds itself. Other companies' needs for information about sales, costs, and profits can be quite different. More often than not, however, some or all of the following reports will be found helpful on a regular (R), periodic (P), or special (S) basis:

Profit and loss statement for the business as a whole (R).

Statements of manufacturing, selling, and administrative expenses (R).

Gross profit (sales minus cost of sales) for major products and/or product lines (R, P, or S).

Gross or net profit for identifiable divisions of the company (R, P, or S).

Various sales analyses (R).

Unit costs of principal products (R, P, or S).

Many executives would also find the following additional statements helpful:

Statements of costs and expenses, according to the executive or department responsible for them (R).

Statement of net profits by major products or product lines (P or S).

Statement of gross and net profits by major customers or classes of customers (P or S).

Statement of gross and net profits by principal channels of distribution (P or S).

Statements of contribution to overhead and profit by products and product lines, customers or classes of customers, channel of distribution, and so on (R, P, or S).

Sales and Cost Classifications

These statements and analyses can be seen to constitute the results of classifying and summarizing sales, costs, and expenses by meaningful criteria to bring out significant relationships. In classifying sales, the following categories are most often used, singly or in combination:

Product or product line.
Customer or class of customer.
Territory or geographical area.
Salesman, branch, or channel of distribution.

In classifying costs, categories such as the following are normally employed:

Sales classification.
Nature of expense (e.g., salaries and wages, materials, purchased services).
Organizational responsibility.
Purpose (e.g., manufacturing or selling).
Pattern of behavior (e.g., fixed, variable, or programmed).

BENEFITS OF COST, PRICE, AND PROFIT INFORMATION

Each of these classifications of expenditures can in some way contribute to the knowledge that the businessman can gain about his costs, about the relationship of these costs to sales, and about total profits and profits from segments of the business. Each can tell him a good deal about what has happened in the past and why, and, in so doing, tell him also something about what may be expected to happen if he takes certain actions in the future.

When the executive uses information about costs, sales, and profits in the past to plan for the future, he may find that some of it will have to be changed to reflect expected changes—for example, if sales prices are expected to change, or material prices to rise, or a new union contract to go into effect. In making these changes, however, he will build upon the past and his knowledge of what has occurred. He will also be able to build upon his knowledge of what must occur if he is to be more successful in the future than in the preceding period.

How can information about costs, prices, and products be used to help management improve the future of the company?

Richard Harris, or any president, can use the information in many ways.

Psychological Stimulus

A knowledge of where the problems lie, and their extent, produces a psychological force, based on economic necessity, that can motivate the president and the other executives to take bolder and less popular actions than they would if they did not understand the reality of the situation.

Budgetary Control

A knowledge of where costs deviate from standards, budgets, and plans can be used by management to exercise a greater degree of control over the manner in which departments and other organizational units comply with the spending or profit plans contained in the budgets. They can measure more precisely the effectiveness with which these units carry out their functions. Thus, a tighter degree of administrative discipline can be exercised than if problem areas cannot be isolated.

Pricing Policies

To the extent that price latitude exists—or, in other terms, to the extent that prices are not established by the actions of the market as a whole or by those of a larger competitor— this information can help to bring about better estimates of those future costs upon which bids and proposals or prices should be based (assuming such a relationship exists). It can also provide better data on which at least target prices are established for old products, for new products, or for new features of both.

Information about costs and profits also helps both executives and the sales force to hold out against unnecessary price cutting or underpricing. It reinforces the degree of resistance with which the executives are able to withstand requests for such actions.

Negotiations with Customers

When prices are, to a degree at least, related rather directly to costs—e.g., in the sales of Harris' unbranded items to a single customer—the possession of valid information about costs can be used advantageously to argue for higher prices.

Capital Investment and Product-Line Decisions

To the extent that there are opportunities to alter the manner in which the company's assets are used, this information serves to bring about shifts to increase profits. For example, it can lead the company to increase the sales of its more profitable products by devoting more of its sales and promotional efforts to them, by keying advertising and sales commission plans to profitability, and by using the company's production equipment for a greater proportion of the time to produce the increased volume of sales. It can lead the company to decide to drop models on which profits are unattractive or non-existent, and to set out deliberately to find or to develop new ones that it can make with better economic results. It can lead a company to set up criteria as to when to abandon a plant, an assembly line, or a piece of equipment, and when to acquire new machinery that either is more effective in producing an old product or can make a new one with a higher rate of return. Through these and other methods, information of this type can tell Harris and his counterparts where they should place their money and their company's efforts to produce a greater return.

Profit Maximization and Exceptions to Policy

To the extent that an opportunity exists to change either prices or the volume of business, this kind of information enables the company to have a knowledge of and then to seek the best relationship of price, volume, and profits in the light of its circumstances. It also can help in deciding when a specific business opportunity, such as a specific order offered at a non-standard price, would contribute to an improvement in profits or produce the opposite result.

Distribution Policies

To the extent that some latitude exists to change the manner in which products are marketed, changes are permitted in the focus of sales or the channels of distribution through which the company reaches its markets in accordance with results. By being able to determine, for example, the comparative results that occur by selling directly to a customer, through retailers, through jobbers, and others, the company is better able to select the focus and method by which it moves its goods to market.

Top-Level Strategic Planning

Finally, executives can use this information in the preparation of plans and in the evaluation of the alternatives available to them, when they are engaged in planning the company's future. Much of the information described in this chapter not only contributes to answering specific questions, but also provides an important insight into how a company's costs and profits can be expected to change under alternative decisions.

Information about costs, prices, and profits is basic to an understanding of current operating results and to planning for improved performance in the future. It is alternately a part of and a contribution to the information by which the questions "How am I doing?" and "Where am I heading?" are answered. It provides a basis for reviewing and taking action based on what has occurred, and what is anticipated and/or planned for the future.

4

Markets, Customers, and Products

THE STATIC SALES-CURVE PROBLEM

"I have concluded," said William Carter, owner of a tool and hardware manufacturing company, "that there is no further point in discussing what has happened. We know what we should do.

"We have been making tools and other kinds of hardware for almost 100 years, and we pride ourselves that we make them well. Our customers seem to like us; by and large we get along well with them. We are not, however, doing very well. Our sales are not rising. Every time we attempt to increase prices we meet with severe resistance, and, with increases in costs, our profits are squeezed.

"My prime interest and experience lie in manufacturing. I could be mistaken, but I seriously doubt that there is anything very much the matter with the level of our manufacturing costs. Since something is obviously wrong, however, we must face the possibility that we have been getting out of touch with our markets and that our products are not as attractive as they used to be. Let's find out what the situation is—where our markets are, who our customers are, and how good our products are."

It is an unusual executive who cannot sympathize with Carter, for the situation that confronts him is one that has applied, does apply, or will apply to most companies at some time and, more likely than not, applies to some products of any company at any time. Products seem to have a life of their own based on the needs or wishes of the marketplace, not on whether a company likes to make a particular product or is efficient in its manufacture.

Carter's problem is thus everyone's problem, and Carter's description of how his company set out to solve it should have universal interest.

"When we first started to think about our situation," said Carter, "we came to the conclusion that the amount of information we could hope to obtain was relatively limited, but that was all right because we did not need to know very much anyway. However, the more we thought about what serves to make a product attractive or unattractive to customers, the more information we decided would be helpful. And, surprisingly, the more we thought about where we might obtain some of this information the more widespread became the sources that we believed would be open to us. As a matter of fact, we began to see that information on markets and products might be so extensive that, like all other information, it would reach a point of diminishing returns."

Market versus Product Approach

"There are at least two ways of looking at the problem," Carter continued. "One of them focuses attention primarily on the customer and the market; the other, on the product. It seemed to us, however, that product and market were so interrelated that both should be included. At any rate we felt that, at the early stage of our investigation, we should not attempt to limit the focus of our questions so sharply as to prevent us from learning what we really might want to know.

"There were a number of questions that we might have asked, but these were the main things we thought we should try to find out:

Who are our customers and why do they buy from us?

Who are not our customers and what are the most logical reasons why they buy from our competitors?

Are our competitors experiencing essentially the same problems as we are, and, if so, do their problems have the same apparent cause and the same indicated solution?

Are our products satisfactory? If not, how can they be improved?

Are there other products that we could manufacture which would use our basic skills and manufacturing abilities, and possibly our same sales force, to increase our sales to our present or additional customers?

Do we compare favorably with competitors as far as prices and credit are concerned?

Is our packaging attractive?

How effective is our advertising and promotion?

How do we stand on service and on the speed and cost of delivery?

Do we give adequate technical support to users or should this be improved?"

Carter and his staff had obviously come to appreciate that a variety of forces and factors contribute to a company's ability to make a sale. They had begun to sense that for a company to be a winner it need not excel in every respect but only on balance, and that what was important to one customer or one class of customers might easily have a different value for another. They had come to see that there are many sources of information available which they had not previously realized existed and that, without even making an attempt, they were exposed to many impressions, facts, and data while carrying out their normal work. They began to see that part of the process of collecting information was just being aware that it was needed and using whatever opportunities they had to gather it.

At this point, several of the executives started to offer ideas on the nature and solution of the problems and to argue the relative merits of the alternatives proposed. Carter listened for some minutes and then stated that, while the questions were important and the suggestions seemed to have been well considered, he felt it premature to decide what should be done and preferred to wait until more information could be obtained about the total problem. He pointed out that since the bulk of the executives' day-to-day contacts was with certain kinds of individuals in a limited range of situations, they might have an unbalanced view of the facts. He suggested, therefore, that they should withhold judgment for a time and try instead to identify sources from which information might be obtained, to specify the kinds of information that might be sought, and to assign responsibility for obtaining what was available.

SOURCES OF AVAILABLE MARKET AND PRODUCT INFORMATION

Information about markets and products is available from a variety of sources. Many of these sources are, of course, incomplete or potentially inaccurate, since they deal only obliquely and incompletely with a company's products and markets. Others have a limited and even self-interested view of the question, which may result in answers that reflect their own desires. Only the skillful selection of important information from all sources will produce a balanced, reasonably accurate answer.

A variety of sources of information will result in an overlap or a conflict in the information collected. While this is often a nuisance and a problem, it is also a strength. Information about the same subject from various sources can be used to check on the accuracy or validity of other information received. It can confirm or override a feeling as to the significance of various characteristics of the product or of the market. It can even tell a good deal about the differences of opinion that exist among purchasing, manufacturing, design, and sales departments within the manufacturer's and the customer's own organizations. Information about markets and products is, in short, characterized by a lack of unanimity which should be expected and accepted as normal.

At the next meeting of the Products and Markets Committee, as the group had by then come to be known, the members discussed the question of sources—where good information about markets, customers, and products could be found. As the discussion proceeded it became increasingly clear that useful information could be expected to come from sources of three basic types: (1) internal sources (the company's own employees and its records), (2) semicommitted sources (organizations with which some kind of a business relationship is maintained), and (3) external (largely neutral or even competitive) sources.

Internal Sources

A company's internal records are a major source of information—albeit a latent one until skillful analysis brings the facts to light. A statistical analysis of inventory and sales records, of credit memos and returns, of current invoices and incoming orders for periods long enough to be meaningful can reveal a number of interesting facts. It can, for example, help to disclose what has been happening to sales of specific products and groups of similar items; whether there is a life cycle to the company's products and, if so, what it is; to whom the company is making the bulk of its sales and the kinds of businesses they are in; trends of prices, credit, and so on. Such a study can tell which sales are moving through various channels of distribution and perhaps tell what happens when a change is made. It can give clues about what happens when the company increases or decreases prices. There is a lot that can be learned—even more now than in the past, thanks to the computer and more sophisticated mathematical techniques. The information will not be conclusive in some areas by any means, but it should give clues and support answers or raise questions about information obtained from other sources. The controller can often do the best job of working with these records, for many of the records are his responsibility; but if he is wise he will consult with marketing and other executives both in setting up his analyses and in interpreting the results.

A company can also learn a lot from talking with its own employees, especially if they are given a chance to do some thinking and investigating on their own before the discussions take place. Salesmen will probably be the most valuable sources, since they are in frequent contact with customers and probably know more about customer reactions to products than anyone else. They have a chance to see what competitors are offering and to find out about their prices and credit policies. They have catalogs, price lists, and other data in their files. They have an opportunity to discuss what can be done to improve their company's own line with the purchasing agents with whom they deal. They are used to thinking in terms of advantages and disadvantages, of strong points and defects. The reasons given by salesmen when they fail to make an important sale are not too reliable. The reasons given may be correct, but chances are that they are not.

Some of the technical men who work with customers should also have valuable ideas. Particularly, they should be able to contribute information with respect to technical performance, desirable features that might be added, new materials that might be used, and additional products that might be made using the company's existing or related technical capabilities. They usually will not discover too much about prices and credit terms, except in those companies where the manufacturing staff plays an important role in specifying the source from which products will be acquired.

The company's own purchasing agents are another useful source, for they see a number of products offered by a wide variety of manufacturers, and thus may be able to provide information about what competitors are offering, about new products their own company might consider manufacturing, or about new materials and techniques that might be usefully employed in their own company's product line.

Finally, there are, in addition to those with frequent direct contacts with the "outside world," those supervisors and staff assistants—including headquarters staffs, product designers, and top executives—whose contacts are both direct and indirect. Their point of view and their information will reflect their experience and opportunities and the nature of their job.

Thus, the major internal sources of information are (1) the records and (2) the employees of a company who, through their normal business contacts with customers and others, are in a position to learn of customer requirements, of product advantages and disadvantages, and of opportunities to improve existing products.

Semicommitted Sources

The second major source of marketing information is that group of individuals or companies with which the company has a direct business relationship. These are not people who are on the payroll, except perhaps indirectly through the payment of fees or commissions. They are, however, people or organizations with an interest in the company's well-being, and often with a great deal of knowledge as well, who would often be willing to make information available if they were properly approached and if someone of reasonable stature and authority talked with them. There are at least six of these semi-committed sources:

Dealers and distributors.
Advertising agencies.
Accountants, bankers, and other business consultants.
Suppliers.
Retailers.
Customers.

William Carter discussed them in the following way.

DEALERS AND DISTRIBUTORS. "Dealers and distributors can obviously help. They handle a wide variety of products which they sell to a number of different customers. They often, in fact, have a better and broader view of their market area than most of our salesmen do. We have some dealers and distributors who handle competing brands or brands that come close to competing with our own. They thus acquire a good idea not only of the strength of our product line but also of the potential that exists for attracting additional customers or additional sales from our own customers by making improvements in our line. Because they tend to concentrate their efforts on a smaller geographical area, they can often give us a pretty good reading on how businesses and business needs have changed in the areas in which they sell. They can give us reasonably good clues about how successful we and they actually are in gaining access to new companies in their area and about the degree of success they have in persuading those companies to buy. Since they receive sales support and technical support from a number of manufacturers, they may be able to tell us how we compare with other companies they represent."

ADVERTISING AGENCIES. "Our advertising agency also can supply us with information and advice that will be of assistance. They make it their business to have a good deal of statistical and other analytical information available about products and markets, most of which they have compiled themselves or obtained from the government, trade associations, and other sources. It is quite unreasonable for someone like us to expect an agency to do a really comprehensive job in this area when you consider that 15 per cent of what we pay them for advertising in a year amounts to less than $25,000. Nevertheless, they can and do give us good advice, using information they have developed to manage our advertising program. They can tell us something of the practices being followed by other concerns. They can make some of their basic data available to us. For an additional fee, they will carry out more extensive market research, if we decide to call upon them for that purpose."

ACCOUNTANTS, BANKERS, CONSULTANTS. "Accountants, bankers, and other similar business consultants—the third of the semicommitted sources—also have some useful comments to make, although usually they are somewhat more general in nature. They frequently have useful information about general conditions in the area, and about recent and impending changes. Perhaps they have the same for our industry. Of course, we would not expect them to reveal anything about their other clients or customers because they have a confidential relationship with them, the same as they do with us. We cannot, to tell the truth, be quite sure that we will obtain in this instance anything that will be useful for our purposes, but we should not overlook this possibility. We at least can obtain a general impression about how effective our efforts appear to them and the impression we make on them as a business enterprise."

SUPPLIERS. "Suppliers can contribute a good deal more information than we might at first expect. When we first considered them as a source of information, I was inclined to be quite skeptical until we talked about this possibility with our purchasing agent and our product-design engineer. They both said something that is entirely logical—that suppliers are very much interested in seeing their customers grow for the same reason that we are: they hope that as their customers grow, these same customers will buy more from them. Since one way of seeing a favorable growth occur is for the customer to have a good line of products, suppliers constantly offer what they hope are constructive ideas, in conversation or through technical literature. They attempt to interest us in using more of their materials in existing, new, or better products. They attempt to show us how and why their equipment should be used. Their 'sales talk' is aimed at pointing out advantages we can gain. What might be considered as self-interest has important elements of mutual value. There is merit, therefore, in talking with the more important suppliers, with both their salesmen and their technical support staffs, to see what ideas can be generated. Of particular value can be those suppliers who, because they are bigger or more specialized than their customers, may have access to greater technical knowledge and/or larger technical staffs and thus may be better informed about what is and will be going on."

RETAILERS. "The stores that retail our products also can tell us much that we can use. After all, they are closest to the customer and more likely to note his reaction, even when they may not be particularly able to interpret it or to do what needs to be done. Especially when one follows the practice of selling solely through wholesalers, dealers, and distributors, it is easy to become isolated from the ultimate customer and try to make and sell products in the light of an image that is faded and past. Stores, their buyers, their clerks, and their customers provide a good antidote to that problem, for their time period is current and their time span is short. The newer retail outlets handling our merchandise, particularly the self-service and discount stores, probably deserve special attention, since there could be distinctive problems in that kind of outlet of which we are presently unaware."

CUSTOMERS. "Finally, we can probably obtain good information from the customers themselves—what they think about our products, specifications, prices, credit, packaging, service, and the improvements they believe we can make.

"It is easy to see why these semicommitted sources might be able to provide valuable information. They have contacts with our products and our markets that frequently permit them to see our problems from a different point of view. They can, in most instances, be expected to have relatively capable staffs

—individuals of stature, experience, and ability who more often than not are willing to discuss our problems with us in a helpful, constructive way."

External Sources

Some sources of information are essentially "external." Their business relationship is slim and their interest in a company tends to be either neutral or competitive. The four major external sources are trade associations, business conventions, publications, and competitors. The first of these may not fall entirely into the category of an external source, since no one could claim a lack of interest on the part of a trade association in its members. Trade associations have, however, been included in this group because they are committed to helping all companies in an industry, not just a specific one. One could also say the same thing about the other external sources.

Many trade associations are active in compiling statistical information on sales and related matters. Some of their reports closely correspond to the business reports of the specific company; even when they do not correspond exactly, however, a company can often find them useful as an indication of what has been happening in the industry as a whole and for comparison of the information received from the association with its own figures. Thus, it can get at least some idea about how well it is doing compared to others and how well various types of products are faring in the market. Trade associations often have excellent material describing what has been taking place in related industries and thus can provide good background material and perhaps some valuable specific clues.

Trade conventions, where papers are presented and products are on display, are also a source of information. Usually one will not acquire any very startling information from them, but shows can produce additional ideas about competitors' products or about other products the company could make.

Another source of information is trade magazines, not only those covering the company's own industry but also those read by the principal customers it serves. In them are found interesting advertisements, some of which describe new products and new production ideas, and technical articles dealing with

products and technologies. Interestingly enough, some magazines, published primarily with the interests of production and
other technical specialists in mind, often contain ideas that an
imaginative individual can turn into new products or into new
uses for old ones.

A good deal of statistical information, particularly about in-
comes, population characteristics, and consumption habits and
trends, is generally available from a variety of business and
governmental sources. Also, it is often possible to buy or to
"borrow" such data from various companies or organizations.

The final source of information is competitors. After all, a
company knows a great deal about its competition. While
much of it comes from outside sources of one type or another,
it is surprising how much information comes from comments
made directly by competitors. Not that companies compare
notes on prices or other matters prohibited by law; but competitors, by definition, have many of the same problems and
do talk, when they meet, about ways in which they are trying
to solve them. Perhaps more important than anything else,
competitors have common problems arising from imported
products, or from the application of new technologies or new
materials, or as the result of changes in the needs of customers.
Some competitors enjoy "playing games," and their information is relatively unreliable. There are always others with
whom a company can have serious and fruitful discussions; but,
as one might expect, these will often be companies who are not
competitors in the same geographical areas.

OBTAINING THE INFORMATION

"Well," said Carter, "if we are to make much progress, we
are obviously going to have to find a way to use our time and
effort intelligently. We are going to have to be selective in
what we investigate, intelligent in what we ask, and careful
in how we interpret what we are told. Unfortunately, this is
not going to be a simple matter of crossing off the appropriate
box on a questionnaire.

"I think that the sales manager should be in charge of getting the necessary information and that we should assign his
top assistant to work with a top technical assistant from the

manufacturing area to pull the information together and analyze it. The controller should analyze some of our internal records, after he has a chance to show the other members of the group what information is available or can be made available, so that he will not do a lot of work which does not fit our needs. I am not sure two or three men can do this job alone, and if you think we need some outside help I hope you will let me know.

"If our studies become larger or we decide to try to find out some more complicated kinds of things, we can consider engaging an experienced outside consultant. We will obviously gain both experience and man-hours in that way. I understand, moreover, that sometimes customers feel freer in talking with third parties than they would in talking with one of our own employees, and that an outsider might very well have a better chance of learning more than we can about some of our problems and weaknesses and of obtaining some constructive suggestions on what we can do about them.

"Let's avoid broadside requests for information. Instead of asking the sales force or the technical staff as a whole for information, select a few and talk with each in depth, and then perhaps ask them to get additional information on the basis of their contacts.

"Insofar as possible, the major part of the knowledge we need should end up in the heads of the group members. Knowledge will build on itself, and things not apparent on the basis of isolated reports or impressions will become more apparent as more information becomes available. You will also be able to sense some of the more subtle relationships, as you get to know more about the problem, and cross-check the accuracy of facts, data, and impressions more easily. Finally, you will have created a small group with which we can up-date this information later.

"Let's also make full use of the trade-association information. We have it, we understand it, it gives us a basis for comparing what we have been doing with the industry as a whole. We should pick and choose among what we call our 'semi-committed' sources, taking a smattering from each group but paying most attention to our dealers and distributors or suppliers, and to our industrial and retail customers. I am not, I must confess, quite as impressed with the initial possibility of obtaining a great deal of useful information from retail stores, and unless you find, on the basis of one or two tests, that these are constructive uses of your time, delay any further work in this area until we see what we can do with our other information.

"I will prepare the requests for interviews, since some of the recipients may respond better to a letter signed by the president of a company. After you make your preliminary selections, let's talk them over."

EVALUATING AND USING THE INFORMATION

Needless to say, all did not go smoothly in the planned study. Carter and his associates were alternately baffled and annoyed by the conflicting nature of what they learned and by the impracticality of some of the approaches suggested. Nevertheless, in due course a semblance of order began to appear, and certain very significant facts began to emerge.

They discovered, for example, that a much larger volume of their products than they had supposed moved through some of the newer kinds of retail outlets, and that their particular form of sales organization was not well set up to handle these customers. They learned that the requirements for some of their customers' products were forcing these customers to turn to products with higher specifications from other suppliers, and that Carter's company was not moving rapidly enough in this field. They learned that some of the newer technologies were actually providing their customers with substantially different approaches to performing the function now performed by Carter's products, and that Carter's company had to either acquire a competence in these different technologies or look for other markets. They found that there had been drastic changes in business opportunities, in either different geographical areas or different industries, in the last ten years and that they had not altered their salesmen's use of their time and efforts sufficiently to take advantage of them. They also found that, while the company had been adding to its line, it had not been eliminating items with falling sales; and that, while customers still continued to order the old items, they were willing to shift to

other of the company's products which served the same purpose. They found that by and large their prices and credit
terms were competitive and that in most respects their standards of service were satisfactory.

A number of customers expressed a desire for additional
technical literature or assistance in helping them use the
company's products, especially the more complicated items.
Finally, they obtained excellent ideas on products that could
be made with essentially the same types of machinery they
presently possessed, to give them a broader and more diversified base. Some of what they learned could be used quickly
and inexpensively; the effective use of other information required more time and more money, and some suggestions could
not be used at all. There were no longer the old confusion and
indecision as to the nature of the situation, and management
could more vigorously and realistically plan its actions for the
years ahead.

Marketing is a major concern in any business. For a company to be successful it is not enough that it be able to design
and manufacture efficiently. The product must be one that
fills the needs of the customers and the marketplace, and it
must be brought to their attention skillfully. It must meet customers' requirements not only in quality, but with regard to
credit, price, service, and technical support. Customers' needs
are constantly changing. Other industries are attempting to
find ways to satisfy these needs. Competitors are constantly
trying to make their products, prices, and services more attractive to potential customers. A company cannot therefore expect to proceed satisfactorily if it has an inadequate view of the
market it is trying to reach or an incorrect view of the attractiveness of its products in that market.

There is a great deal of information available from sources
within the company, from other sources with which the company has a well-established business relationship, and from outside neutral or competitive sources. With the expenditure of a
reasonable amount of time and effort, a businessman can obtain
a good deal of valuable information. He will usually find, in
fact, that his biggest difficulty is not in obtaining information,
but rather in selecting that which is pertinent, correct, useful,
and worth the cost.

Information about products, customers, and markets is of value not only in terms of the present and the immediate future, but also in terms of a company's longer-range plans. It is, as we have seen, one of the mainstays of the whole planning process. Marketing, as Carter's experience has shown, can be effectively approached by developing and using sound and realistic information.

5

Inventory and Production Management

Frank Loring, the president of Mid-West Novelty Company, a small manufacturer of toys and novelties sold mostly in hardware and variety stores, called a meeting to discuss for the umpteenth time what was wrong with inventories. The warehouse was bulging; yet late shipments and back orders were frequent, and customer complaints were building up. The salesmen were upset because promises were not being kept. The controller was annoyed because inventories were sopping up more and more of his cash. The manufacturing manager did not like the short runs and the expedited shipments. The purchasing agent spent most of his day pleading with suppliers for fast delivery. Everyone's nerves were on edge and something had to be done.

Loring clearly had a problem. What had happened? Inventories had grown out of line with requirements for manufacturing and for sales. Why? How could information help Loring to do something about it?

FUNCTIONS OF INVENTORIES

The management of inventory is, for most businessmen, a matter equal in importance to and often of greater difficulty than the management of cash. Cash can be used for a variety of purposes. Inventory, and more particularly each item in it, is an asset with a much more limited use. Therefore, consideration of the nature and purpose of inventories, of key problems of inventory management, and of the importance of information in solving inventory problems should be of value.

Inventories—raw materials and purchased parts, work in process, and finished goods—constitute a large portion of most companies' assets. There is no question that inventories are necessary; it is useful, however, to define exactly what the functions of inventories are:

They are a substitute for time. Inventories make it possible for a company to manufacture and deliver goods more quickly (because items already on hand can be used) than if the company had to wait for them to be made or bought and delivered.

They serve to reduce costs. Inventories make it possible for goods to be bought, made, and/or delivered in larger quantities than are immediately necessary and thereby permit goods to be made, bought, sold, and delivered at lower costs.

Well-managed inventories would have permitted Loring to give more efficient customer service, to schedule manufacturing more effectively, and to purchase goods, materials, and services at a more attractive price. Poorly managed inventories did just the opposite—they led to out-of-stock or wrong-stock situations, to poor scheduling that antagonized customers, to increased operating costs and obsolescence, and to forced purchases made at disadvantageous prices. Inventories, because they are at the core of his business, affect the entire operation of Loring's company. Poorly managed inventories may themselves be the result of managerial problems; whether they are or are not, however, they certainly cause problems of all sizes and kinds when they exist.

INFORMATION MOST USEFUL IN MANAGING INVENTORIES

Inventories, although they are one of the most "physical" assets of a company, are particularly dependent upon the quantity and quality of information available about them and they are peculiarly vulnerable when that information is inadequate. Most decisions involving inventories are based on what records say about them, not upon what is learned by a physical examination or count of the items themselves.

The proper management of inventories requires a variety of information. What this information is and why it is useful can be clearly seen by looking more closely at the functions of inventories: saving time and reducing costs. By being available, inventories make it possible to make, deliver, and sell more rapidly and with less effort than if they were not available. To perform these functions, however, the specific items on hand must include what the customer (whether he be the plant or an outside customer) wants, and they must be available when he wants them. Wrong items or out-of-stock items are no help.

Inventory management's fundamental responsibility is to come as close as is practicable to having the right things available at the time they are needed, and to do this within the financial and physical constraints that good inventory policy involves. This requires a combination of factual knowledge with estimates and projections. In tackling the problem, it is usually found necessary through some combination of techniques to:

Estimate the future demands for products. This requires a forecast of future sales and inventories, and an analysis of orders on hand.

Write up the specifications of the materials and parts going into the final product.

Prepare production schedules based upon the forecasted customer and inventory requirements and product specifications and efficient manufacturing practices.

Create a reporting system giving the status of production, inventories, and backlog.

Analyze the financial costs of carrying inventories.

Each of these will be explored in some detail.

Estimates of Future Demands

All businesses rely to some degree on estimates of future demands, whether they "make goods to order" or deliver them "off the shelf." Companies expected to give off-the-shelf service must rely heavily on predictions of future demands if they are to have the goods available when required. Many other manufacturers, even when permitted to deliver days or weeks after the receipt of an order, must also rely heavily on predictions of demand, since the delay permitted is not adequate to allow the manufacture of the products from scratch. It is even apparent to those acquainted with "make-to-order" industries that what their customers consider a tolerable manufacturing and delivery period will often require that they keep inventories of raw and semiprocessed materials on hand. Estimates of future customer requirements are thus of use to all manufacturers, whether the prediction is (1) a relatively pure forecast, with comparatively little to go on, or (2) largely a compilation of orders "in the house," or (3) a combination of these.

FORECASTS. Let us first consider the forecast. Loring's forecast is a prediction of the future made on the basis of estimates of future demand rather than on the basis of concrete evidence. It rests on the collection and interpretation of information gathered from the sources indicated below:

Information	*Probable Sources*
About the past:	
Sales of this or similar items by the company	Sales analysis—own records
Sales of the same by the industry	Industry statistics
Sales by close competitors	Purchasing agents, salesmen, etc.
About the present:	
Status of orders and inventory	Own inventory and order records
About the future:	
Extension of trends about past sales	Sales analysis—own records
Executive actions (advertising programs, design changes, etc.) that will help or hinder sales	Own management
Customer requirements	Customers, salesmen, industry publications, market studies
Reactions to new products	Customers, test marketing, initial demand, executive judgment, reception of similar items in the past

Most companies preparing forecasts start with estimates made by the sales department and adjust them in the executive office in the light of additional knowledge of plans and of general or specific conditions that they may know about. In a small number of companies, top executives make the initial estimates and discuss them with sales, manufacturing, and other department heads as part of the "process of review." Other intermediate methods are also frequently used, with economic, marketing, and other assumptions made by top management or its staff advisors being given to those responsible for making the more detailed and/or the overall predictions. The main point, however, is that no matter what the precise techniques, an intelligent consideration of data and plans by persons in a position to know will result in forecasts of demand that can be used, even though they will have to be adjusted in the light of future events.

The degree to which a forecast will be relied upon to establish how much of a product to make and carry will vary, but it will usually depend upon how long the customer will wait after he decides he wants to buy. Toys, for example, might be available on the spot, and thus reliance on forecasts would, in such a case, be relatively heavy. For oil burners or engines a reasonable wait is usually more acceptable, and forecasts are, therefore, not so important or developed to the same degree. If a forecast is to serve only as a general indication of how busy a plant will be, it can be general and contain a fair margin of error. If, on the other hand, it is to serve as the basis for placing purchase and manufacturing orders or for deciding how much of a specific item to keep on hand, it must be more soundly based and precise. Both the detail and precision of the forecast are therefore determined by its intended use.

ORDERS ON HAND. The second major basis employed for predicting future requirements is the analysis and compilation of orders on hand. To the extent that requirements for future sales and production are based on orders on hand, with some adjustment perhaps for orders known to be en route or expected to be received soon, the prompt and accurate analysis of orders rather than the preparation of the forecast becomes critical.

Making this analysis is not usually an inherently difficult task. How effectively it is done, however, is in large measure determined by the skill of the sales and clerical staffs, by the presence or absence of order recording and order entry systems that promote both speed and accuracy, and by the interest evidenced by management in having this analysis made correctly.

The effectiveness with which orders are entered and analyzed is to some extent related to the nature of the product being ordered. Accurately recording and entering new orders is obviously more difficult when the product is technical and complicated and provides for numerous variations and options. It is even more difficult when the order is (1) in some major sense incomplete—with major decisions as to specifications to be made at a later date; (2) for an experimental product as yet only partially designed; or (3) readily cancellable or postponable up until a specified date. Checklists and well-designed forms intended to detect errors, omissions, and inconsistencies can help with the first situations; more sophisticated solutions can only help, but not solve, the problems encountered under other circumstances.

Even relatively simple orders and products are, however, often improperly handled for lack of the proper attention and tools. For lack of adequate catalogs, codes, and sales literature, products are inaccurately or incompletely described by purchasers and salesmen alike. For lack of well-designed forms, essential data are omitted. For lack of well-organized routines, incoming orders are improperly controlled, investigated, edited, entered, and analyzed. For lack of emphasis by important officials, the whole process is treated casually, without regard for its importance in the inventory management process.

For that portion of the requirements for future sales and production which is to be based largely on orders, the analysis must be made not only correctly but quickly. Experience will show that the sooner information about an order is known, the sooner it can be released for purchase or manufacture and the greater the time available for these purposes before the required delivery date. It is surprising how often what was really "lost" time can be "found" by shortening the order-entry process.

Part and Material Specifications

The next of the critical items of information is the specifications of the materials and parts that go into the final product. Without these, it is virtually impossible to tell a vendor accurately what is being bought from him or to tell the plant what it should make. While the more detailed specifications may be incorporated in blueprints or engineering drawings, a summary description of the items used should be contained in what is known as a "bill of materials."

Many companies have "bill of materials" records but do not use this information effectively to improve inventory management, either because they fail to use the system as it should be used or because they permit it to be contaminated by inaccuracies.

Part of Mid-West's problem, for example, resulted from letting the bills of materials get out of date. This is very easy to do if substitutions and other changes go unreported or if inadequate efforts are made to change the master lists. If bills of materials are to provide information for effective inventory management, they must:

1. Reflect actual operations.
2. Contain a carefully prepared description of what the part is.
3. Contain a number that identifies the item throughout the plant and in dealings with suppliers and with customers for spare parts.

A summary of all of the bills of materials, with the duplications eliminated, provides a list of all the parts purchased, made, or assembled by the company. Arranged in a logical order, they become a parts and materials catalog which can be used extensively by the engineering and purchasing departments, by the plant, by the sales department, and even by customers, for several reasons:

Since the catalog contains both a description and a number for each item, it serves as an exact shorthand designation of the lengthier and more technical details.

Because the list of materials is prepared to show the models or products for which a particular item is required, a "where used" list results.

As a result of the list's containing an indication of possible substitutions, a "substitution or alternate" list is automatically prepared.

Since the catalog indicates which items are to be considered standard and which are not, a device is created to prevent an unnecessary increase in items at the product-design stage and to provide an orderly method for introducing engineering design changes and other improvements in products. Deletion from the catalog or the use of an appropriate symbol provides an automatic signal that an item which was formerly standard has been designated as non-standard or obsolete.

Production Schedules

With information about customer requirements and the specifications of the materials and parts going into the final product, the next step is to determine total requirements by periods, and, after adjusting for inventories, to schedule production by periods so that parts and products will be available in the quantity needed and at the time required. To do this effectively requires that there be available information about the capacity of equipment and assembly lines and about the length of time required to perform various operations, as well as about the current status of inventories, orders, and work in process.

With this information, and with more detailed information about when the material or parts will be available so that the work can actually be performed, departmental or machine loading schedules can be prepared and manpower requirements established. Customer requirements in terms of quantities and promised delivery dates can then be integrated with manufacturing capabilities—admittedly a process involving a certain amount of trial and error—to produce a schedule showing what should be done and when. Just how detailed these schedules will be and how often they will be revised will be largely determined by the nature of the business and the characteristics of the product.

Throughout the establishment of both the overall and the more detailed manufacturing schedule, information plays an important supporting role. Virtually all of the data mentioned are expressed in numbers—dates, capacities, and volumes—which must be calculated, analyzed, and arranged to develop the desired plan.

Periodic Status Reports

Another kind of information that is vital to the improvement of inventory management is that which reflects the company's position at a given point of time: information showing how much is on order, how much is on hand, the current status of production, the workload lying ahead, old and new estimated customer delivery dates, quality problems and many other similar facts.

Loring decided he needed a periodic status report. At first, this proved to be difficult and costly to prepare, for although more clerks in both the plant and the office were working on such records than on records of any other kind, the records did not lend themselves to meaningful summarization. Surprisingly, they often were out of balance with each other because of errors, failure to communicate changes to all concerned, and different time spans involved. It took some work to set the records and procedures right and to impress upon employees the importance of speed and accuracy. But, in the long run, the response was good and the information worth the effort in terms of improved operating results.

Financial Data

The final type of information found useful is financial data concerning what carrying different amounts of inventory may entail. This kind of information helps primarily in determining how much of a specific item should be kept on hand. It is clear from the above discussion that many factors are involved in making this decision and that some of them indicate the advisability of carrying large quantities, whereas others argue in favor of small inventories. By using carrying costs and estimates of other kinds of costs and values, management is able to come close to resolving this problem.

A number of mathematical techniques have been developed that attempt to resolve this question in fairly precise terms. Businessmen often apply these to their largest and most critical items, and frequently to those of intermediate importance as well. Simpler techniques involving less precision also help in making the necessary choice. Here is how Loring approached this decision.

Loring, like most small businessmen, elected to make his decision about inventory levels on less than precise grounds. Nevertheless, he took the following considerations into account:

Certain factors favoring large inventories:
Less likelihood of being out of stock.
Greater chance of lower purchase or manufacturing costs.
Lower purchasing and administrative costs.
Certain factors favoring small inventories:
Lower storage requirements.
Smaller chance of loss from partial or total obsolescence.
Lower cost of financing the smaller investment.
Lower insurance and taxes.

In some instances, Loring drew the needed estimates directly from price lists and similar sources, or from accounting records; in other instances special analyses were needed to develop them.

By attempting to assign at least rough values to these and other factors in terms of his circumstances, Loring found he could better assess the net advantage or disadvantage of having large or small inventories of specific items. He thus applied in general terms the same line of reasoning that managers in larger companies would apply more precisely by more scientific techniques.

AREAS OF OPERATING PERFORMANCE IMPROVED BY GOOD INVENTORY MANAGEMENT

Other kinds of information can contribute to the effective management of inventories. The information already noted, however, about forecasts, orders, specifications, capacities and schedules, current status, and the relative values of different inventory levels provided Loring with what he needed most of the time. The same should be true for most other businessmen.

The question then becomes, "How does this help to improve operations?" To find the answer to this question it is helpful to look at the impact of better inventory management on various areas of the company.

Condition of Inventories

Good inventory management clearly can be beneficial to manufacturing, purchasing, and sales. What impact, however, does it have on inventories themselves?

In the case of Mid-West Novelty Company, good inventory management reduced (1) the number of different materials, parts, and finished products carried, and (2) the total amount of cash invested in inventory. Surprisingly, Loring found the total amount of cash invested in inventory was reduced even though prior chronic shortages might appear to indicate that prior inventory was too low, for it was imbalance (too much of one item and too little of the other) that was usually at fault.

What are some other advantages? Loring's experience shows that reducing the number of items carries with it great advantages. It reduces both the number of individual storage bins and the total amount of storage space required. It reduces the number of orders, receipts, inspections, and shipments involved. It even reduces the total quantity on hand, for the safety stock requirements of closely related items, such as dolls' legs, arms, and heads, are always greater than the safety stock requirements for molded soldiers even when the combined consumption is the same.

In the future, Loring hopes to obtain further reductions in the number of items inventoried from a standardization program starting back with product design. This should lead to even greater advantages, for the chances of complete obsolescence will diminish, and the opportunities for substitution in case of shortage will increase.

Looking beyond the advantages realized to date and the future programs visualized, a further overall reduction in the total investment in inventories can probably still be achieved by (1) better sales forecasts or order compilations, (2) better records of current status, and (3) the application of more precise financial data to a determination of the levels at which inventories should be stored. Better sales predictions and order analyses will permit a narrower margin of safety and tend to prevent building up inventories of temporarily or permanently unwanted items. Better records, giving a good fast picture of what is available, will enable the company to react quickly and to give itself ample inventories without building up larger stocks. Financial data showing the high cost of carrying large stocks of high value items may suggest that it will be practical to shift toward more frequent ordering to bring about lower carrying costs.

Thus, the net result of reductions in the number of items or total values invested in inventories is fewer losses from obsolescence, smaller storage and financial costs, and lower tax and insurance costs.

If the value of establishing and maintaining inventories at their proper levels were restricted solely to the reduction in the number of items or the total investment, this alone would often be enough. However, as has been noted, a substantial additional value results from the ability to keep operations moving smoothly, which will not exist when inventories are not in proper balance with needs. Having a large investment in inventories does not necessarily produce the right result. The important requirement is that the money be invested in the right items in the right amounts.

Manufacturing Activities

Having the right quantity of a product on hand when it is needed can have a beneficial effect on manufacturing costs. When the part is available, production can proceed without interruption. When it is not available, or available only in fits and starts, production will be delayed not only on the assembled product but also on any other item of which this product is an integral part. Stop-and-start production will result in more lost time, more setup time, and an all-round reduction in efficiency because runs are short. There may be difficulties with quality and quite possibly higher inspection costs. Parts either withdrawn from the stock room or manufactured and held on the production floor pending arrival of the missing item may become lost or damaged in the interval. When delayed parts do become available, the production of the product may have to be expedited, with a disruptive influence on other orders which would otherwise proceed in a scheduled fashion through the plant. There will certainly be higher production scheduling, expediting, and controlling costs. The availability of the part or item can have a major effect on manufacturing efficiency.

Good inventory management made a positive contribution to Mid-West Novelty's manufacturing effectiveness. For example, with better information Loring was able to schedule facilities more tightly and to achieve a higher rate of production per unit of productive capacity and per dollar of employee wage. To achieve this goal his staff received information about the capacity of the physical facilities as well as the status of inventories and orders on hand and in process. This same information helped to monitor and change rapidly the production scheduling and control system by which the original operating plan was developed to reflect new conditions. The proper use of good information thus helped to insure that the right order and the right material were brought to the right work station at the right time, with the opportunity for the desirable results that this procedure provides.

Finally, good information about how production was going —the volume or rate of speed with which products were being produced, the relative quantities of good and bad, the backlogs at specific points—brought to Loring's attention those areas where action was required.

Purchasing

Better inventory management improves the quality of purchasing, which in turn helps to bring about better inventory management. The one is, to a great degree, dependent on the other. Good information is essential to both. Mid-West's experience illustrates this relationship.

With better information Loring now does a better job of predicting inventory requirements. Loring predicts sufficiently in advance to permit a well-organized purchasing function to exist. This information is used by the purchasing department to do a better job of selecting vendors on the basis of quality and price with less attention paid to speed of manufacture and delivery. By purchasing in larger quantities, the company often obtains better prices.

Better inventory management reduces the number of purchase orders that must be expedited, permits the buyer to spend more of his time on the creative aspects of his job, and brings about fewer canceled orders, with the direct costs which these often involve and the indirect problems of dealing with vendors under such circumstances. Better inventory management also leads to the use of standard items wherever possible, thus reducing the number of items to be purchased and the difficulties encountered when parts are in short supply, or become surplus or totally obsolete. To the extent that the company's inventory management permits it to acquire materials with fewer quality problems, there are also fewer claims on suppliers with which to contend.

Good purchasing, on the other hand, has improved Mid-West's inventory management by helping to have the right materials available on time. It has resulted in the selection of vendors who provide that combination of on-time delivery of specified materials of good quality and low cost which best reconciles the advantages or disadvantages that individual suppliers may have in particular areas. By so doing, purchasing has contributed to keeping the plant on schedule and to meeting the quality and delivery requirements of the company's customers at a low cost.

By playing this role, the company's purchasing department has become more than a clerical pool transmitting requests for purchases from engineers or from plant schedulers to vendors. To do this, they had to receive information about lead times and be informed of shifts taking place in the market during different seasons of the year or at other times. They needed to know the quality and delivery performance of various vendors with respect to different classes of items. They needed to know which orders are in danger of not being delivered in time to meet the production schedule or in time to meet the customers' requirements, so that they could follow these up. They had to provide information to those concerned with plant production and customer deliveries that enabled them to modify the production or delivery schedule in time to do the least amount of damage. Without this information the purchasing department could not have helped to achieve better inventory control through better purchasing.

An effective purchasing department will anticipate strikes and other changes in the markets in which they purchase. It will keep aware of impending price changes in at least the principal markets in which it buys. A good purchasing department will also do "creative" purchasing, keeping its eyes open for new materials which it can suggest to those who are responsible for product design. It can similarly keep alert for requests to purchase non-standard materials or parts and can call to the attention of the proper executives the problems involved.

Thus, it can be seen, there is a relationship between effective inventory management and effective purchasing that makes them interdependent at the same time that it makes both dependent to a substantial degree on the prompt availability of good information.

Sales

Better inventory management contributes to increased sales and customer satisfaction. To see why this is so, consider a few of the consequences of both poor and good inventory management. When poor inventory management existed, the company's ability to sell was hampered in several ways:

1. "Off-the-shelf" sales were often lost forever if products were not available; even those sales not expected to be delivered immediately were often lost if the period before delivery was considered too long by the customer.
2. Customers were lost for future sales when promised dates were so unreliable that the availability of parts or products for their own production or sale could not be counted on.
3. The cost of production was pushed to a point where lower profits had to be accepted or higher prices charged.
4. The excessive use of non-standard parts and non-standard designs complicated the customers' and dealers' spare parts problem and the difficulties of maintenance.
5. The good, often the better, salesmen did not like to stay with the company because they felt they were selling products at a competitive disadvantage.

With good inventory management, an opportunity to improve sales performance is present:

1. Sales can be made because products can be delivered promptly and not, with excessive frequency, be found to be "out of stock."

2. Customers can be gained and held because products are delivered by promised dates or, if they cannot be, the customer can be given a new promised date on which he can count.

3. Spare parts and maintenance problems are simplified by making maximum use of standard, interchangeable parts.

4. The low incidence of delivery and quality problems will give the sales force confidence in the products and service it is asked to sell.

Average inventory management can make a company competitively average; good inventory management can give it a competitive edge.

Administration

Good inventory management contributes to better overall administration. It can be said that inventory (good or bad) moves on paper in the guise of schedules, reports, and forms. Bad inventory management can be caused in part by inadequate or poorly prepared "paper." Bad inventory management will almost certainly, however, also add to "paper." It will bring about a proliferation of schedules, reports, and forms created in an attempt to cope with problems. For example, at Mid-West Novelty bad inventory management resulted in:

Smaller orders.

Back orders and delayed shipment notices and reports.

More purchase orders.

More customer inquiries.

More expediting of purchasing and production.

More purchase and customer invoices.

More receiving and inspection reports.

More complex production scheduling and control systems.

More "hot item" or "red flag" reports.

More conferences and meetings to straighten things out.

Good inventory management can never eliminate all of a company's problems and "extra" administrative work. What it did do for Mid-West Novelty's management, however, was to keep the number and size of the problems small enough so that they could be more quickly identified and brought under control. Just as problems with inventories increase in importance because of the leverage exerted by these problems in other areas, so, too, do improvements in the management of inventories increase in value at a rapid rate.

6

Cash Management

One morning in early June, Jim Thomas, president of Williams Aerospace Company, sat down with his controller, Larry Perkins, to discuss how to meet a pressing and surprising problem. The company, with sales and orders at an all-time high was, to put it bluntly, broke. Payments to suppliers were being deliberately delayed; vendor evasion was becoming a finely developed art. How could this possibly occur at a time when the company was booming and its prospects had never seemed brighter? What had happened?

After a two-hour session and a fair amount of self-recrimination for their stupidity, the two men concluded that what had struck them had been a combination of events whose net effect was that their cash was almost gone. A new product had sold much better than they had anticipated, necessitating a sharp increase in inventories and accounts receivable to support these sales. Inventories had gotten out of line on a group of items with falling sales for which they had failed to decrease production rapidly enough. The accounts receivable credit and follow-up systems had not functioned effectively, and two big customers had fallen behind. A capital expenditure proved difficult to finance, so it was paid for out of "available cash." To make matters worse, the bank was understandably reluctant to renew or expand its loans until the company produced some figures showing how the squeeze had come about and how the company was going to work its way out of it.

Growing, changing, even declining businesses come upon unexpected cash problems with such frequency that the whole story has more than a faintly familiar ring. Sometimes forecasting, planning, and control—i.e., cash management—can do little or nothing to avoid cash crises. Many more times they can. Proper cash management based on good information and good planning techniques can make an important contribution to preventing crises, to anticipating and reducing their impact when they do occur, and, most importantly, to insuring that sound operating plans are not hobbled by cash shortages.

KEY PROBLEMS IN MANAGING CASH

A businessman can feel reasonably sure that he is managing his company's cash effectively if he:

Knows how much cash he will need.

Knows when he will need it.

Knows how much cash he will receive or can obtain from what sources and when.

Adjusts his spending plans realistically as soon as he finds that funds will not be available.

Obtains and maintains the right amount of cash—not too little to a point where the lack of cash hinders progress or poses operating problems, nor too much to a point where excess cash is not put to productive use.

Recognizes that cash is a temptation as well as an asset and takes steps to protect it from theft.

These criteria are straightforward enough. It would seem, therefore, that virtually all companies would do a reasonably good job of handling their cash. Why is this often not the case? What, for example, had happened to Williams Aerospace during the last five years? The answers, in retrospect, were reasonably clear:

1. Thomas and Perkins had not accurately predicted their requirements for and their receipts of cash. In fact, they had not really tried to do so.

2. They had not realized the great effect that changes in the volume of business, the introduction of new products, capital expenditures, and other corporate events could have on the flow of cash.

3. They had an inadequate method of warning them of impending difficulties.

4. They did not have an organized way of adjusting their plans to conform with the realities of the cash available to them.

5. They did not maintain relationships with banks, suppliers, and other creditors that would facilitate borrowing cash, financing payments, leasing items, or raising additional shareholder capital from present or potential shareholders.

Under rather urgent conditions, Thomas and Perkins sat down to try to make up for past sins.

Determining Cash Requirements

The first step in managing cash is to determine how much cash will be needed and when. If Thomas had prepared the budgets and projections described in Chapter 2, he would have been able to start with an annual cash budget and a long-range cash plan. Furthermore, he would have known that since these cash plans were prepared as part of an integrated plan, they would tie in with the actions contemplated in his company's operating budgets and capital expenditure plans. He would also have had a high degree of assurance that the basic cash plans were reasonable, for he would have known that the company's present cash position and its future outlook were both given consideration when the operating and capital expenditure plans were being prepared.

Thomas and Perkins did not believe in budgets and forecasts and had no reliable financial plans—for operations, for capital expenditures, or for cash. After a few abortive attempts to prepare "just a cash forecast," they reluctantly concluded that they needed all three just to be able to forecast and manage the flow of cash. They found that under pressure they would have to rely on less precise and less informed predictions of the future, but that even these had to be developed by the normal planning approach—using data about the past, thinking of their intentions about the future, considering the impact of external influences and internal constraints, and taking into account contemplated executive actions. While the chances were strong that their estimates would lack something in the way of accuracy, at this point they really had very little choice.

In due course, Thomas and Perkins produced a set of what they felt were reasonably reliable plans. From these they obtained the basic information required to project cash expenditures for operations, for capital expenditures, and for a number of financial or other special items such as dividend payments, payments on long- and short-term loans, irregular contributions to pension and profit-sharing plans, and legal settlements. The total of these, they felt, constituted the cash requirements of Williams Aerospace for the next twelve months.

Choosing the Cash Budget Period

Cash requirements expressed in annual terms were, as Perkins soon noted, great for a start but, if they were to be any use to him, they had to be estimated for far shorter periods so that he would have the necessary cash available at the proper time.

As he said, "The problem with looking only at the year as a whole is that it does not reveal the troughs and peaks that result either from seasonal and other changes in the flow of business or from a variety of other major business events, such as major equipment purchases for cash. It smooths too much out of sight. It reminds me uncomfortably of the man who drowned when the average depth of the river was two feet. For this to work properly, I think we'll have to break down our cash requirements by months or quarters, or a combination of months and quarters, or perhaps a combination of months and quarters and years. Initially, at least, I'm going to make up a two-year plan broken down into three individual months plus three quarters plus one year. I'll roll it forward at least semi-annually."

Thomas challenged, "Why do you think you don't have to budget for periods shorter than a month? Why a month—with us so short of cash?"

"Good question," was Perkins' response. Obviously, for now, we're going to have to be very careful with all the cash we have. For the long pull, though, I believe a month will be just about right. It is short enough to take care of the ups and downs arising from our major periodic or special cash expenditures; it is also long enough to reflect our seasonal needs. Maybe I'm really playing with words, but I don't believe that in the long run we will need to or try to predict the flow of cash within a month, or within a week, with sufficient precision far enough in advance to call it planning. I, of course, know payroll dates and vendor payment dates and can easily adjust for those things. I would prefer to think of handling cash for these short periods primarily as 'doing' rather than planning so that our cash plan can deal with trends and events of more importance.

"I hope our cash balances will have some leeway in them in time. Until they do, however, we clearly will have to do a lot of short-term planning and scheduling just to keep everyone even reasonably happy."

Handling the Lag Between Outlays and Receipts

When Thomas and Perkins began to translate their operating, capital, and other expenditures into cash requirements and attempted to allot them to relatively short periods of time, they soon encountered another set of problems centering around the "lag."

Business is not conducted on a cash basis, and cash, more often than not, does not change hands either at the time the transaction legally occurs or at the time it is recorded in the accounting records. The lag affects both the buyer and the seller but, in most instances, it seems to affect the seller more seriously.

A teen-age baby sitter, collecting cash from her client as she prepares to go home, is in one of the few businesses where a lag in the flow of cash does not exist. Most businesses can hardly expect to be in that fortunate position.

Perkins, upon studying the flow of funds in his company, found that the planned outgo of cash preceded the planned receipt from sales by anywhere from days to months, depending on the terms of sale and the customer's paying record. He discovered that before his company could receive much in the way of cash from customers, or for that matter from anyone other than shareholders or general creditors, it must expect to incur an obligation for substantial amounts of cash for at least the following:

The plant and equipment with which the product is to be manufactured.

The materials out of which the product is to be made.

The salaries and wages of employees and the goods and services of others required to manufacture and sell the product.

The costs of administering the company's affairs, paying taxes, and so on.

He knew he could reduce his cash outflow by paying for some of these obligations on a delayed basis involving months or years but, even after making adjustments for this, his budget showed a net outflow of cash. Therefore, he decided this had to be given careful consideration in budgeting cash both over the long haul and within shorter periods of time.

How the lag works in practice can be seen rather dramatically in the Williams Aerospace Company when it was first established. At that time the company had the following rather simple characteristics:

Capital expenditures were financed by a long-term monthly payment loan.

Suppliers required that materials and other items be paid for approximately thirty days after the receipt of the goods.

Employees were paid on a weekly basis on the Wednesday following the end of each week.

Its only product took about two months to manufacture.

It sold to its customers on thirty-day terms.

The table shown below indicates how cash flowed in the company during its first four months of operation.

	January	February	March	April
Cash Required for:				
Loan Payment on Plant and Equipment	$ 5,000	$ 5,000	$ 5,000	$ 5,000
Materials		15,000	15,000	15,000
Payrolls	10,000	10,000	10,000	10,000
Taxes	10,000			10,000
Other Expenses		5,000	10,000	5,000
Total Outlay for Month	$25,000	$35,000	$40,000	$45,000
Total Outlay to Date ..	$25,000	$60,000	$100,000	$145,000
Cash Received on Sale (shipped in March)				(85,000)
Net Cash Required to Date	$25,000	$60,000	$100,000	$ 60,000

Several items are worthy of note.

Although the February 28 balance sheet showed the inventory cost of the product was $80,000, payments of only $60,000 had been made by the time its manufacture was completed at the end of February.

At the end of each month, the balance sheet listed unpaid bills of about $20,000, mostly for materials and other expenses. Taxes were also owed in different amounts, although they were required to be paid only on a quarterly basis.

The cash required to be invested in inventory and receivables to support one sale every second month peaks at at least $120,000.

The plant and equipment mortgage still remains substantially unpaid.

This situation is typical of that found in many companies, irrespective of whether they are just starting or well-established. Substantial amounts of cash must be invested in plant and equipment, in inventories, in receivables, and in other costs or expenses incurred in selling the product and running the company. There is, therefore, a permanent lag which varies in amount in relation to the volume of business and the speed with which cash moves out of and into the company.

As long as the volume of business of a company remains about the same, a businessman should have little difficulty in using his company's prior cash experience to predict his future needs. He should and usually does have relatively little difficulty in predicting variations in cash requirements due to regularly recurring seasonal changes. He is most likely to stumble when, like Thomas, he does not realize that changes are taking place, or when he incorrectly judges their impact. Some typical changes of this sort are listed below:

A substantial, nonseasonal change in demand.

Different methods of distribution requiring greater inventories, such as when branches are established or warehouses are built.

New standards of customer service requiring that the supplier maintain higher inventories to provide faster delivery.

Different credit terms for a new type of customer.

A new line of products with different manufacturing characteristics.

In each of these situations, the timing of the lag is likely to be altered and/or the amounts of cash involved increased substantially. Therefore, they must be handled with particular care.

Cash expenditure requirements, which may be stated by way of summary, can be determined by:

The proper estimation of operating and capital expenditure demands.

The proper prediction of special financial requirements.

The proper identification and use of information about lags.

These three factors combine to produce the first half of the cash budget: the determination of cash requirements.

Estimating Cash Receipts

Determining how much cash will be received and when is the second half of the job of cash budgeting. This requires separate, essentially unrelated estimates of (1) when the company's customers will pay their bills, (2) receipts from investments and other miscellaneous sources, and (3) other sources from which the money will come. The first and third of these will be discussed separately. The second is self-evident.

COLLECTIONS FROM CUSTOMERS. Using his prior estimate of sales, Perkins had little difficulty in estimating the amounts to be collected from customers. He determined when the money would be received by applying past statistical trends to his estimated credit sales and by then making adjustments for expected differences. His basic assumptions using past trends were that bad debts would be 2 per cent of sales, and that sales would be collected in an average of forty days.

The approach and format eventually adopted by Perkins usually suffices for most businesses.

Perkins made some further adjustments for such factors as advance payments from customers; future bad debt losses he felt to be material in amount, due to the condition of specific accounts, to a general decline in business conditions, etc.; and known differences in the paying habits of such customers as governmental units. The first of his cash receipts predictions was thus completed.

	Estimated Cash Receipts from Sales (*thousands of dollars*)					
	Jan.	Feb.	March	April	May	June
Accounts Receivable —Beginning of Month	$60	$68	$64	$ 92	$128	$214
Sales	55	45	75	100	175	100
Collections	(47)	(49)	(47)	(64)	(89)	(147)
Bad Debts Written Off						(11)
Accounts Receivable —End of Month	$68	$64	$92	$128	$214	$156

FINANCING FROM OUTSIDE SOURCES. Perkins found making the third estimate—those amounts that could be and should be obtained from outside sources—considerably more difficult. It involved (1) determining, on the basis of the type of need, whether long- or short-term funds should be sought; (2) determining whether from the standpoint of corporate policy or the wishes of the owners these sources would be acceptable; and (3) deciding whether, under the circumstances, these sources would probably be willing to lend money or to invest.

Perkins determined whether short- or long-term funds should be sought from a review of his proposed operating and capital and cash budgets and of the balance sheet itself. In preparing his cash budget, he followed the normal procedure of:

1. Establishing cash requirements for operations, for capital expenditures, for dividends, for repaying prior borrowings, and for other purposes.

2. Estimating how much cash would be provided from operations and from ordinary vendor credit.

3. Establishing the net deficit and then deciding the sources from which these funds would come in view of the nature of what brought about the deficit.

Thomas and Perkins considered the various sources of funds that might be open to them and prepared the following table showing the circumstances under which they would be inclined to consider each one.

| | Indicated Solution | | |
	Short-Term Borrowing	Long-Term Borrowing	Shareholder Equity
If the shortage:			
is temporary (even if recurring seasonally)	x		
is long-term:			
to support operations		x	x
to acquire plant and equipment		x*	x
would make the current ratio dangerously low		x	x
would make the equity/assets or the equity/debt ratio dangerously low			x

* Possibly also sale and leaseback arrangement.

Thomas and Perkins then considered corporate policy implications involved in the different choices, and roughly concluded:

1. If the funds are to be provided by trade creditors, there will usually be few if any corporate policies involved, unless the suppliers offer to lease the equipment or to provide long-term financing of some other sort for capital expenditures.

2. If the money is to be acquired from banks, factors, bond and mortgage moneylenders, sellers of conditional sales contracts, and similar sources, they, and perhaps the board of directors, too, will need to consider the amount of long- and short-term debt that is desirable, particularly in relation to the shareholders' investment and the willingness of the company to lease instead of to buy.

3. If shareholders are to provide the funds, either through additional stock investment or through retained earnings, they and the board should consider the relationship of shareholder investment to debt, dividend policy, the willingness to share ownership with others if present owners cannot provide funds, and even the determination of the size and scope of activities of the company itself.

After considering a number of factors, Thomas decided to seek bank financing. To finance his seasonal working capital he wanted a six-month loan. To finance some substantial equipment purchases, he hoped to obtain a five-year term loan. His cash budget indicated he could repay the working capital loan with the cash "thrown off" by the normal contraction in inventory and accounts receivable which followed his peak sales. The budget also showed that the five-year loan could probably be repaid out of the cash generated by operations, as long as dividends were not raised.

At this point, having decided on sources and amounts on the basis of the cause of the impending cash deficit, the condition of the balance sheet, and corporate policy, the big question remaining became the willingness of the investor or lender to provide the funds. Whether this must be determined in advance of preparing the cash budget is a matter of business judgment, in which such considerations as previous use of this source, previously expressed attitude, and probable attractiveness of the opportunity to investor and lender will undoubtedly play a part. The obvious minimum objective, which was what Thomas sought, was to gain reasonable assurance that the plan was practical.

PUTTING THE CASH PLAN TOGETHER

Putting the cash budget and the long-range plan together was now not difficult. It involved essentially a further extension of basic plans into shorter periods and more detail about the sources and expenditures of funds.

In its final form, the company's cash budget appeared as shown on page 95.

COMPARING ACTUAL PERFORMANCE WITH THE PLAN

A cash budget is, it can be seen, a combination of plan and prediction. As such it serves the same purpose as other plans and predictions. Once the budget had been established, Thomas and Perkins were in a position to compare it with actual results and to take corrective action. If they noted that the cash position was less favorable than anticipated, they might have discovered that inventories were being purchased in advance of the time required, that inventories of slow-moving

Cash Required:
Capital Expenditures ....
Dividends ....
Payment of Long-Term Debt ....
Payment of Short-Term Debt ....
Special Expenditures ....
Operations: ....
  Payrolls ....
  Materials ....
  Manufacturing Costs and Other Expenses Exclusive of
    Depreciation ....
  Income Taxes, etc. ....
      Total Cash Required ....

Cash Provided:
Balance from Prior Period ....
Short-Term Loans ....
Long-Term Loans ....
Shareholder Investment ....
Operations:
  Sales and Other Income ....
      Total Cash Provided ....
      Balance End of Period ....

items were building up, that bills were being paid in advance of due dates, that expenses were not being controlled, or that other things were being done or not done to contribute to a slowing up of receipts or an acceleration of expenditures. They might then decide to take actions that will correct the conditions indicated, or to alter their plan by postponing certain expenditures or by changing either the sources of funds or the amounts to be obtained from them. With a plan and a comparison of actual results, they could probably discover the potential difficulty sufficiently in advance to be able to prevent, or at least lessen, its impact.

HOW TO USE INFORMATION IN CASH PLANNING

A good cash plan results from the intelligent application of good information. It is both a result and an extension of a basic planning process which depends heavily on information. It relies on information about actual results to indicate when conditions need to be corrected or the plan amended. It both uses and is information. The experience of Williams Aerospace illustrates this point.

Generative Cash Within the Business

Cash may be generated—at least temporarily—by a decision to postpone an expenditure, such as the acquisition of a piece of machinery; to postpone introducing a new product; or to delay the start of an advertising program. It is more likely to be generated, however, by reducing the investment in inventory, by stretching out the payment of bills, or by more promptly collecting accounts receivable. Some of the actions taken by Williams Aerospace illustrate this point.

Perkins found that the reduction of investment in inventories was one of the most fruitful sources for the internal generation of cash. Individual items and groups of items were studied in relation to current and historical trends, the requirements of current production, and predicted sales. Purchasing practices and policies with respect to safety stocks were re-evaluated. Where better information was needed, it was obtained; where better practices were required, they were developed and applied. The net result, as is so often the case, was the ability to operate a business with a reduced inventory of purchased and manufactured materials and parts, an inventory of finished goods in better balance with customer requirements, and a corresponding increase in cash.

Perkins also improved the flow of cash by speeding up the collection of accounts receivable. He did this in various ways, such as changing some aspects of the company's basic credit policy by altering discount terms for prompt payment and by increasing the speed and persistence with which customers were billed and followed up.

CREDIT POLICY. A decision as to whether a customer's business should be accepted will often be determined by his credit rating. It is well known that too tight a credit policy will unduly restrict sales, and that, conversely, taking credit risks serves a useful function in promoting sales. Thus, it might be said that some sales are made in spite of the fact that there is a recognition that slow payment or even non-payment may be involved with a particular customer or class of customers. Such customers require that persistent efforts be made to obtain funds from them as promptly as possible, and that credit limits be closely applied when determining whether additional shipments should be made. At times, recognition can be given to the fact that some customers take longer to pay by adding a penalty for delayed payment or by providing a discount for prompt payment, by selling to them only on a C.O.D. basis, or, alternatively, by working out an agreement with a financial institution by which such sales can be handled on an installment basis.

BILLING PROCEDURE. At times, it is possible to speed up the flow of cash by changing the manner in which the customer is billed so that the invoice will reach him and be approved at an earlier date. Since customers will usually not pay without an invoice which has gone through a proper approval procedure in their own company, considerable care should be taken (1) in preparing the bill and sending it promptly to the customer and (2) in so designing the bill that it will contain the information (e.g., the customer's order number, shipping date, etc.) the customer needs to check it out and approve it for payment quickly. Many companies make it a practice to pay vendors' invoices one, two, or three times a month to minimize the number of checks they have to draw. Thus, a delay in the receipt of an invoice or a problem encountered in approving it may well result in a disproportionate delay in the receipt of the funds.

Many companies also have approval systems that result in approving bills in proper order rather quickly, but involve substantial delays if the invoice must be diverted for special investigation. Thus, the basic system for invoicing can play a part in the speed with which cash is collected. So, too, can the quality of the work performed by the billing clerks. Although the system may be excellent, if invoices full of errors are produced, severe problems will obviously be encountered.

FOLLOW-UP SYSTEM. Accounts receivable can also be collected more rapidly if the company has a good follow-up system and uses it effectively. In part, a system must rely upon the skill and abilities of the employees who carry out this work. Their effectiveness can, however, be increased if the records and information produced for them are such that they can tell which specific items are outstanding, rather than only the total amount involved. Their efforts will be more effective also if accounts can be aged to show which are current and which are past due. With this information, collection efforts can be directed toward accounts in difficulty or to individual items about which there are problems. They can give priority to those accounts where the greatest amounts are at stake or where the company's credit rating indicates problems may be encountered. They can pay greater attention to seeing that the customer does not become overextended in the first place. An executive possessing information of this nature, in summary form or in more detail about key accounts, can also follow the efforts of his credit manager more closely with a minimum expenditure of time, and thus bring about an improvement in the status of the outstanding accounts.

OTHER APPLICATIONS OF INFORMATION. Cash can also be generated internally by watching more closely the credit terms offered by suppliers, for frequently a company will, through habit or carelessness, pay its vendors without regard to when the bills are due.

Information can also help to identify probable amounts of excess cash and to reveal when that excess is large enough to warrant being invested or placed in short-term treasury bills, certificates of deposit, savings accounts, or other interest-earning investments. Without adequate and accurate information about when, how much, and for how long funds will be available, such a program can be both a nuisance and an embarrassment. With it, excess funds can be turned into an earning asset.

Cash, it is clear, can be generated or, to be more precise, untied through actions taken as a result of the proper use of information.

Obtaining Cash from Outside Sources

Information can also be used to secure cash from outside sources. Often, as a cash budget is being prepared, management will recognize that sufficient cash will not be generated from customers or other internal sources to meet the requirements for cash in the periods ahead. The executive, unless he is to change his plans, will have to look elsewhere, to creditors and shareholders.

Most outside sources of cash must be approached formally. This means not only that the discussion will be serious and to the point, but also that the prospective borrower will have to show the prospective lender or shareholder enough information to convince him that (1) he represents a good risk, (2) the purposes to be served by the loan or investment are sound, and (3) the probability of repayment or of a satisfactory return exists. This usually requires that information about past performance and future plans be presented. Even where this is not required, it is clear that a substantially more favorable impression will be made if such data are available. A person with a clear idea as to what he has and what he intends to accomplish and a plan to which he has given thought will quite logically find it easier to present his case than if this information is not available to him. Since final approval to obtain the funds frequently is given not only by individuals present at a meeting, but also by others who are not, the existence of well-organized information will help to assure that the executive's story is transmitted correctly and in full. There is even an advantage to discussing information on performance and plans with potential lenders and with owners when money is not immediately required, since this will help to develop a relationship that will make funds more readily available when they are needed. There is certainly value in doing this with banks from whom money is regularly borrowed.

In all of this, the businessman should realize that a prospective lender or investor will not merely judge the facts but will also reach some conclusions about the quality of the executive as a manager. Prospective lenders and investors have frequently seen the consequences of the failure to plan and the lack of adequate knowledge about what has been accomplished; they can hardly feel as happy with the prospects of lending to or investing in a company whose management gives little visible evidence of being capable in these areas as with a company whose management not only knows how to plan and control, but also has available physical evidence of it.

By way of illustration, the experience of Thomas is of interest. Fifteen months after the situation described at the beginning of this chapter, Thomas and his controller put together a set of financial statements for each of the past two years and a set of the plans that had been worked out for the next several years, as well as a cash budget for a proposed new product line. In the cash budget, the specific amount needed from the bank was identified and its use explained. After a discussion with the banker, at which these statements and plans were the center of attention, and after further study on the banker's part, he called to say that he would recommend approval to the loan committee. In due course, the loan was granted.

The next time he was at the bank, Thomas reminded the banker that a little over a year ago his request had been rejected under conditions at least as favorable as those that existed now, and that he had obtained only about half of what he had needed, and at a higher cost, from another source. The banker said the reason for this was rather clear; he had been unconvinced that Thomas really knew what to do with the money and how and when he would be in a position to repay it. He acknowledged that maybe the rejection had been wrong, but pointed out, "The rejection was right on the basis of what you gave me to judge. As a banker I must judge the probability of repayment when due, and there is an obvious reluctance to do this when no numerical evidence is offered that repayment can be made, and when there is not much evidence to indicate that management has thought the matter through. It is every lender's right to ask for and receive properly documented information which will assist him in making a decision concerning the propriety of a specific loan request. Borrowers who cannot or will not meet this request for information often know that they cannot justify a loan and probably should not receive one from a prudent bank. Borrowers whose purposes and condition justify a loan often unwittingly place themselves in the same category."

7

Delegation and Control

DELEGATION OF RESPONSIBILITIES

Robert Scott, president of Scott Electronic Parts, Inc., paused at the door of his office at 11 P.M. one Friday night. Almost involuntarily he turned, smiled somewhat ruefully, saluted, and said, "See you tomorrow; I guess that's what weekends are for."

It had not always been this way. Some five years before when Scott and his principal partner, Russell, had started out, they had not had much more than a little capital and the determination to make high-quality electronic subsystems. From the beginning, Russell had been the man with the electronic and engineering ideas, and he had succeeded in developing one product after another with a batting average sufficiently high to achieve the kind of reputation for technical excellence that had been one of the firm's original goals.

The company had prospered, sales had increased, and business had grown to the point where the staff numbered about 150 employees. The managerial and administrative problems had kept pace—cash, inventory, manufacturing, and selling problems had increased to the point where what had once been a relatively simple task threatened to engulf Scott. Scott, who, except in the field of design, had been from the outset virtually a one-man executive force, found that there were not enough hours in a day for him to do what needed to be done.

The fact was that Scott actually was pushing himself to a point where he threatened to do as much harm to the company as he had previously done good. He had reached the stage where problems were building up more rapidly than they were being solved. Things that needed to be done today were being postponed, not just until tomorrow but until next week and next month. In an attempt to deal with matters that he really had neither the time nor the energy to consider, Scott started to make decisions whose quality left something to be desired. Scott had reached a point which every executive in a growing business reaches at some time—the point where he must learn to delegate and control.

Necessity for Delegation

Scott really had only one alternative open to him—to delegate some of his duties to others and not to proceed on the mistaken assumption that he either could or needed to do everything himself.

The position in which Scott found himself is a common one, characteristic of small companies, of smaller units of large ones, and in a modified way of units of any size. All find that as they grow they reach a point where the old managerial structure with decisions and responsibilities centered in one or relatively few individuals must be superseded by one in which responsibilities are more widespread. There comes a point when, no matter what their energy or capabilities, one, two, or even a small group of executives will run out of time. The inability of a single executive to deal with all or virtually all managerial problems may be caused by an increase in the size of the business, in the number or complexity of its products, in the number, classes, or geographical areas of customers served, or by any one of a number of factors that serve to make the business more complex.

Most businessmen have such a driving desire to grow and prosper that they arrive at this critical point as much by choice as by the force of circumstances. It is possible to recognize the point that cannot be passed without jeopardizing the old form of management, and some executives may choose to hold down the size of their company and to restrict its complexity to a level below that point. More often than not, however, the danger line will have been passed before it is recognized, or it will be passed in spite of the intentions of the executive. When this occurs, it is most unlikely that the process of growth or complexity will be reversed.

One of the most important days in a company's history arrives when the president appreciates the very simple and significant fact that unless he chooses to share his responsibilities with others he will be an obstacle to effective operations or put a check on his organization's growth, and that he will limit his ability to train his own successor in the art of management unless he is willing to delegate some of his authority and responsibility.

Reluctance To Delegate

If the necessity to delegate authority is so self-evident to others, why does a problem exist? Why should there be any reluctance on the part of the president? The reluctance or failure to delegate or, conversely, the practice of retaining all significant responsibility in oneself can usually be traced to the existence of one or more of the following:

1. The fear that a subordinate will not be sufficiently capable to handle the duties assigned to him.
2. The fear that a subordinate, although capable enough, will make decisions based upon an inadequate or incorrect understanding of the company's policies and plans.
3. The fear that responsibility that has been delegated can no longer be controlled.

There may, of course, be a certain degree of validity in each of these fears, and it might be said that many executives would, if they could avoid it, be just as well off if they did not have to make this choice. If a president had the time and the energy, he probably could do a better job than the subordinate to whom authority and responsibility have been delegated. On the other hand, since these are not the facts, and since the time and energy are not available, to act as though they were constitutes an unwarranted action which can only be a serious stumbling block to the success of the business. It certainly underrates the advantages of delegation. The only comparison that can be fairly made is between (1) the performance of an executive who lacks the time and energy, and (2) the performance of a subordinate who has the time and energy to perform his part of the job.

How, then, can the president approach the problem of delegation?

BASIC APPROACHES TO DELEGATION

A president who is setting out to assign duties and responsibilities to key subordinates usually finds that he has several choices open to him.

AREA OF DELEGATED AUTHORITY. He can choose the area for which he wishes to make the subordinate responsible. Thus, the responsibility can relate (1) to the function that the man is to perform—such as marketing, manufacturing, or finance, or (2) to some separately identifiable part of the business, or (3) to a specific branch, territory, or other geographical area. The point about all three forms of assignment is that the delegation of authority can be made in such a way that the powers granted to various individuals and the results of their operations can be clearly identified.

AMOUNT OF AUTHORITY. He can choose how much authority he wishes to give to his subordinate. He can choose to give complete or relatively complete authority to him within the area assigned, or he can limit the authority given for various kinds of actions that the subordinate may be called upon to take. The executive could, for example, give the subordinate authority to hire and fire employees up to a certain level, but require that for higher-grade employees similar actions be taken only after discussing the matter with him. He might choose to give the subordinate the right to spend money for operating purposes as long as he stays within the departmental budget, but require that all capital expenditures over a given amount be referred to him and possibly to the board of directors for approval.

DEGREE OF CONTROL. The president also has a certain area of choice about how and to what extent he will attempt to see that the delegated authority has been properly exercised and the responsibilities properly carried out. The president may rely upon visual observation and discussions with executives and with others, or he may rely upon information contained in reports. Most probably he will do some of both.

The president may also choose whether to review and control the actions of his subordinate on a detailed basis or in more general terms. If, for example, the subordinate is operating on a budget, the president may choose to hold him responsible for not exceeding any of the specific expenses listed in the departmental budget. On the other hand, he may choose to permit the subordinate a degree of latitude and require only that he not exceed the total budget for the department. He may even decide, where circumstances permit it, to measure, review, and control the responsibility of his subordinate solely on the basis of the profits that the department or division earns, or on the basis of the rate of return that these profits represent in relation to the investment required to support those activities.

It can be seen, therefore, that a president can choose not only how to assign responsibilities and how much responsibility to assign, but also how he wishes to measure, review, and control the manner in which these responsibilities have been assumed.

THE ENABLING ROLE OF INFORMATION

Before responsibilities can be reviewed and controlled they must be understood. For a man to carry out his responsibilities properly, the following are important:

1. He needs to understand clearly what his responsibilities are, and the degree of his authority in discharging them.
2. He needs to understand the company's policies and objectives so that he knows in general terms what the company is trying to accomplish and within what limitations action can be taken.
3. He needs to know what corporate plans are, specifically enough so that he knows what is expected of him in terms of income, expenses, and results.
4. He needs to know how well he is doing in terms of the results he is expected to achieve.

Thus, what the subordinate needs to know to carry out his responsibilities properly is exactly what the president needs to know to feel comfortable in assigning these responsibilities.

Information can play an important part in making the delegation of authority both practical and effective. It can be significant in making sure that the person receiving authority has an adequate and correct understanding of the company's plans and objectives, and that he understands the areas in which responsibility is being delegated to him and the amount of authority with which he has been entrusted. Information in the form of adequate reports will help to provide the president with a basis for exerting control as well as to know the manner in which the authority is being used. Indirectly, it can contribute to the development of subordinates by permitting them to learn how to manage through making decisions within the areas and to the extent assigned to them.

It is clear that numerical information alone cannot completely provide either an understanding between the president and those to whom he delegates or a basis of control. An understanding of the objectives, policies, and conditions within which the company operates must be transmitted in a variety of ways. Much of the kind of understanding that is important in preparing a budget and a long-range plan will serve also to indicate goals, plans, and responsibilities to those who will have to help carry them out. Thus, there is value in having those to whom substantial authority will be delegated participate in the development of plans, or at least in discussing plans with them in sufficient detail so that they are clear.

The principal value of numerical information is that it adds precision. If the president were to say only that he wished to see sales increased substantially, those listening might have widely different interpretations as to what "substantially" meant. One executive might think 25 per cent, another 15 per cent, another 10 per cent. However, as soon as numbers are used—percentages, units, or dollars—a more precise statement can be made; differences become clear and can be resolved. Similarly, when a president says that "costs might increase moderately," or that "the competition might lift prices to some degree," he can make his meaning clearer if numbers are used.

With numbers, particularly when they are arrayed in the form of a budget or a plan, the president can reach an agreement with those to whom he is delegating authority about what he expects each to accomplish. These agreements may cover a number of different areas—sales by product lines or territories; share of the market; expenses for a branch or a department; total or unit costs of production; sales, expenses, and profits of a division; or the return on assets invested in the business. Both the president and those to whom he is delegating authority would then know what the president expects.

With numbers, the degree of delegation can also be controlled. If a man is given the right to approve capital expenditures of a "moderate" amount, moderate can be defined as not exceeding $500 or $1,000. If a subordinate is given certain responsibilities for granting credit, a cutoff figure can be established beyond which he must refer the question to the president for approval. With such dual controls—the one provided by the budget or plan and the other by the degree of authority granted for specific types of transactions—numbers can provide a concrete basis of understanding to which both parties can agree in advance.

The net effect of this specification of authority is to make the delegation complete within the limits established and thus free the president from direct participation in those events that do not exceed established limits of authority. Equally important, the person receiving the authority has a basis for proceeding with most of the things he is expected to do without the necessity of referring matters within his province to the president. In addition, a basis is established upon which the performance of the subordinate can be judged. The man with a clear idea of what his authority is will not feel that he is being asked to proceed with one set of objectives in mind only to be judged retroactively in the light of another set of goals.

Since the degree of authority and responsibility delegated to a subordinate can be fixed in terms of dollars or numbers which are rather precise, the president can also, with numbers, vary the authority in accordance with the capability of the man to whom the authority is assigned. He may wish to reserve approval of proposed advertising expenditures to himself because they are unusual in nature or large in amount. He may also wish to reserve this control because he does not believe the sales manager has sufficient knowledge, skill, or judgment in this area, although he may be fully competent to handle other activities carried out by a sales force. He may decide to give the right of approval of capital expenditures to one manager up to a limit of $500, but either because of the character of the activities or the greater experience of another manager be willing to increase that authority to $1,000 or $2,000. The president may at one stage of a man's career be unwilling to grant him authority that he will be willing to grant when the man has become more experienced in the areas assigned to him. Thus, the delegation of authority can be measured and made more flexible and better adapted to the circumstances through the precision gained in using numbers either in the form of dollars or other units.

ESTABLISHING A CHAIN OF COMMAND

Scott quite fortunately learned most of this. He discovered:

To grow beyond a certain point, he had to develop an organizational structure and a chain of command so that he could assign responsibility to other individuals.

He had to provide these individuals with an understanding of the goals and objectives of the company and its policies in general terms, and supplement this general understanding with plans and budgets which set forth these goals and objectives in more precise terms.

He had to assign to various individuals the responsibility for carrying out certain portions of the plan on a basis that was complete or that was shared with him or some other executive in a clear, well-established manner.

Certain kinds of activities carried out by his subordinates did not require individual attention or approval in advance on his part, but other kinds of actions were of a nature or of an amount which made it important that he approve them before action was actually taken.

With reports, and information from other sources, he could tell how well the activities were being carried out in the various areas assigned to his subordinates and could improve their performance when this was required. Conversely, he found he had a basis for praising performance when this was warranted.

Certain employees who had been extremely capable were not able to assume the responsibilities of acting in a managerial role at the outset; they had to be encouraged and trained to take on additional responsibilities. Some employees succeeded very well, others only in a mediocre way, while still others were unable to do what was required of them. Those who did not demonstrate managerial capabilities had to be assigned to jobs in which this skill was not required.

Scott therefore undertook to implement his program of delegated authority and responsibility. He prepared statements of authority, responsibility, and organizational relationships for himself and for each of the executives and their departments. He discussed the basic philosophy of the program and the specific statements with each of them, separately and as a group. He had the budget broken down organizationally so that each man knew his expenditure authorizations and limitations, and he arranged for actual results to be reported on the same basis for purposes of comparison and control. Scott worked out measures of performance—volume, price, growth, share of market; return on investment and profitability; inventory turnover; etc.—and obtained agreement that they constituted fair bases for determining whether a good job was being done. He established a capital-expenditure approval program and set dollar limits on certain other types of expenditures that could be made without his approval. Finally, he set up a formal procedure for reviewing corporate and departmental results, establishing a regular schedule of meetings for that specific purpose.

FREEDOM TO MANAGE

Scott found that once he had broken away from the limitations of essentially one-man rule, there were few if any further organizational limitations on the size or complexity of the company that he could not overcome. The process of subdivision and delegation might have to be repeated as one area became too large or too difficult for one subordinate to manage alone, but the process involved was no different from that which he previously had carried out successfully for the company as a whole. Scott found himself increasingly able to determine, through the use of numbers, important facts about the company's progress and problems which he previously had been able to understand only through personal participation in the decision or through discussions and visits where he could "see things with his own eyes." He found that, with his combination of planning, delegation, and control, he could effectively manage a larger and more complex business by concentrating his time and attention on basic issues and basic objectives and upon those areas of the business that were not performing as effectively as they should be. He had freed himself not only from details but also from giving his attention to all the areas that were proceeding at least as well as planned. In short, he had become a manager.

8

New Forces Affecting
the Role of Information

During the past decade or so, several forces have appeared that have had a visible impact on the form and content of information and on some aspects of its role in the managerial process. These are:

1. The electronic computer and its associated communications equipment.
2. The combination of mathematical techniques and scientific method, often called "operations research."
3. The increasing emphasis placed on planning by business executives and governmental officials, and the new problems and techniques associated with planning and managing large military, scientific, social, and political projects.

Each of these is a major force in its own right. Each also forms part of a whole environment of innovation and change. Each has tended to make information more useful and more important. Consequently, it would appear worthwhile to consider how each is affecting present ideas about information and may affect the future.

ELECTRONIC COMPUTERS AND
COMMUNICATIONS EQUIPMENT

Electronic computers and their recent ally, high-speed communications equipment, constitute the first and most highly publicized of these forces. Their significance is derived in part from the sheer power of electronic data processing (EDP) equipment, which has made it possible to do things that were either physically or economically impractical in the past. EDP equipment has without question greatly facilitated the processes of recording and gathering data, of manipulating it, and of delivering information to those who can use it. In addition, computers have had an impact because data processing has attracted many highly qualified persons who otherwise would have had little or no interest in this field. These individuals have come to data processing with different backgrounds, different experience, and fresh and inquiring minds. It is not surprising, therefore, that they have often viewed the whole problem of how to handle information in a new light and have created new ideas and techniques and new uses for information itself.

There are many ways of looking at the impact of electronic computers. Taking the overall viewpoint of this book and looking at how computers are affecting information from the point of view of the general business executive, it can be concluded that the major impacts of computers have been:

1. To reduce the cost and increase the accuracy of information.
2. To increase the speed with which information becomes available for use.
3. To assist in the coordination of interdepartmental activities.
4. To facilitate the extension and supervision of delegated authority.
5. To increase the opportunity to centralize and/or decentralize operations.
6. To increase the accessibility of information to the decision maker.
7. To increase the risks involved in developing information systems.

Cost and Accuracy of Information

The first impact of computers has been in reducing the cost of handling and processing raw data and improving the speed with which information is produced. This has been accomplished primarily through improving the manner in which clerical and administrative work is handled at its lowest and more detailed levels, and secondarily through extending the scope of mechanization to clerical and semiclerical activities which had been performed manually in the past.

By and large, solid sound results have been achieved. Whether they have been particularly earth-shaking has seemed to depend on the size and type of company involved. Usually, the improvements have been most striking when the work to be accomplished was complex and the volume of transactions was large, although sometimes only the latter requirement needed to be met.

It is important to add that these improvements—reduced cost, increased accuracy, and increased mechanization—have often had substantial secondary values, for they have provided a base that has made other accomplishments possible. Without increased accuracy, an ability to enlarge the amount of data in "machine sensible" form, and a low processing cost, many of the other impacts of computers would not have occurred.

Speed of Information Availability

Because EDP-based systems have been able to record, transmit, and process data much more rapidly than was possible in the past, they have been able to reduce the period of time that elapses after an event has occurred and before information about it is made available to someone who can use that information. This reduction in elapsed time has made it possible to improve the quality of short-term planning and control, and thereby, through a combination of faster reaction and more informed decisions, to provide better customer service and to bring about a better utilization of manufacturing facilities, manpower, and other corporate resources. Obviously, if information is made available more quickly, a company can react sooner, and thus have a greater period of time available in which to take corrective action. Conversely, if a company wishes to delay action until the last possible moment, it can do so with a greater knowledge of the existing facts.

Companies are finding increasingly that with the help of EDP they can produce critical information on work loads, inventories, orders, commitments, and other subjects more rapidly than they could in the past. Faster information, since it arrives in time to permit management to take more effective action, thereby clearly serves to facilitate the management process.

Coordination of Interdepartmental Activity

Computers can also help to bring about more effectively coordinated action as a result of their ability to supplant duplicated or partially duplicated records, currently maintained by various sections or departments, with one centrally maintained electronic file to which all units will have access.

Decentralized, duplicated records seem to have certain inherent problems—partially because of their cost and partially because of their seemingly inescapable tendency to be in disagreement, in error, or out of phase. As such, they are a frequent source of wrong or inconsistent action, or of inaction. When there is a single, accessible electronic record, there can be greater assurance that the information will be more accurate, more complete, and more up to date because (1) the record can be checked electronically for inconsistencies and for incomplete information, and (2) the inadequate but costly prior efforts to maintain several records can now be concentrated on maintaining an accurate, up-to-date record.

A good electronic record increases the likelihood that all departments will take the correct action at the proper time. Because departmental actions are taken on the basis of the same information, the odds are increased that they will be properly coordinated. Perhaps departments will be notified by the computer itself as to when to take action and what action should be taken. As a consequence, management should have greater assurance not only that day-to-day actions are more effective, but that managerial policies and practices are more consistently applied.

To a great extent, the benefits thus far discussed affect the work performed and the decisions made by the lower levels of management and by their supporting clerical and administrative staffs. As such, they relate primarily to responsibilities for the planning and execution of those day-to-day operations most extensively delegated by top management. In such instances, the benefit of EDP to top management is largely indirect: if a better job is done at the lower levels, there are fewer problems for top management. Other benefits, which are at least somewhat more direct, may also be expected to accrue to top management. These are discussed in the following sections.

Extension and Supervision of Delegated Authority

Computers, to the extent that they help to assure that delegated operations are correctly carried out, can help to make delegation safer and/or provide a basis for making it more extensive. To the extent that computer-based records more clearly and more quickly indicate when the delegated power is and is not being effectively discharged, they also serve to protect the integrity of the process of delegation by improving the quality of the supervision provided. The former they do because improved, coordinated information, made available more rapidly to all who need it, should produce better decisions and better results. The latter is accomplished by the production, more cheaply, rapidly, and accurately, of information that shows how well things are actually going—information supporting the process of control. This information comes in the small business largely from the analysis and summarization of detailed records; it is more often than not a by-product of the maintenance of those records, obtained by a relatively insignificant additional effort. The same is also true in large enterprises, but the results have often been less useful and more expensive because of the amount of time and money this "additional effort" involved. One of the great advantages of EDP to the manager is the opportunity it provides to analyze, summarize, and otherwise manipulate the detailed records of the company to produce information that can effectively control the exercise of delegated power.

Opportunity to Centralize and Decentralize

Computers can, in conjunction with high-speed communications devices, provide management with greater freedom of choice as to whether to centralize or decentralize managerial functions in a geographically decentralized enterprise. One of the reasons—often the most compelling reason—for deciding whether to delegate specific kinds of authority to managers of geographically separated units has been the availability of adequate information at the specific location. The information required to take appropriate action dictated what could or could not be done. The new combination of computers and communications equipment modifies this to some extent; in fact, it will often provide a previously unavailable alternative, since information formerly available only at outlying locations can be made available centrally. By overcoming the problem of distance, it becomes almost as practicable to participate in making certain decisions with respect to the operation of a unit 1,000 miles away as one 1,000 feet away. This obviously makes centralization a more practical alternative than it has been in the past.

Conversely, this same combination of data processing and communications equipment can make decentralized management more feasible by making available to the decentralized units information that heretofore was not available to them. Such information may relate directly to the decentralized unit itself, but it is more likely that it will relate to other units of the company—to information about inventories, available manufacturing capacity, customer credit status, etc., in other units or in the company as a whole. Thus, the decentralized manager can make decisions with adequate knowledge of their impact not only on his own unit but also on the larger interests of the company.

There are economic factors involving the cost of communications that restrict the number of occasions for and the types of decentralization that are desirable. Also, there are other managerial considerations of both a tangible and an intangible nature that come into play. Nevertheless, it is possible and, as examples in existence indicate, at times advisable for top management to shift the locus of authority when the availability of information ceases to be the controlling factor.

It seems most likely that a shift will be made toward centralization (1) when the types of decisions required to be made by local managers exceed their capabilities or the information that can reasonably be made available to them, or (2) when the need for or advantage in operating the company as a single unit rather than as a set of units is accompanied by the necessity of choosing one of several alternative courses of action on the basis of a knowledge of current, frequently changing circumstances.

It seems most likely that the shift will be in the other direction when the implications of the action to be taken are essentially local, when most of the information required is needed only at the local level, and when the information provided from the central point need only contribute to the quality of the decision rather than form the specific basis for it.

How extensively the opportunity to centralize or decentralize functions will ultimately be used is uncertain. Some feel that the total impact will be large and some that it will, on balance, be small. The important thing would seem to be that the availability of information, with the assistance of computers and communications equipment, has opened up new patterns of organization to fit the needs of the situation.

Accessibility of Information to Decision Makers

Computers, it can be clearly seen, will some day make information considerably more available to management. The television screen, supported by banks of electronically stored data, will become a useful reality. The result will be, at least for many years to come, far from "push-button" management, for what appears on the screen can be no better than what is available in the "data banks"—the files of electronic data—behind it. What will be in those banks ultimately, no one yet knows; it depends on the questions management asks and the skill and cost involved in supplying the data. Initially, it can be expected that the data may be somewhat orthodox, designed to make more available the information which management and its clerical support already have but which is to all intents and purposes "locked up" in some record or report or file, for all the use it is to management at the time when the subject on which it bears is under discussion. Making this information more available by making it available on call may well have a more remarkable effect than one might expect. When the base is small, increments to it are proportionately large.

Risks Involved in Developing Computer-based Information Systems

Looking at things from a negative point of view, top management can be pardoned if it feels it is caught in a bit of a trap. Improvements in information processing and information utilization do not come easily, cheaply, or without the assignment of a staff with appropriate talent and skill. Minor improvements are not too difficult or expensive to achieve, but, by definition, they do not accomplish too much either. Changes that improve corporate and managerial effectiveness in a major way are, however, another matter. They are not easy or cheap. They can only be developed by people with substantial skill. They require a large expenditure of time and money, and even then they are often speculative. They are hard to install, develop "bugs," may or may not work as well as anticipated. Often, however, they accomplish a lot, even if some of the results are not directly measurable. If an advantage accrues to a competitor by his success in this area, it will not be quickly or easily overcome.

Generalizations do not apply to specific situations but to aggregates; if one were to generalize, however, it could be said that the more aggressive, more successful companies generally decide that improving information processing and utilization through the use of EDP is sufficiently important to warrant a substantial allocation of talent and resources. This is probably, at the moment, as good a measure as there is.

Computers and Small Business

Before leaving this discussion of computers, a few comments about the relationship of EDP to the small business are appropriate. Some years ago, this subject could have been easily dismissed, for the options available were few and their attractiveness minimal. What has changed matters has been the appearance of (1) smaller and less expensive, yet useful equipment and (2) the service center, complete with powerful equipment and, at times, with appropriate programs, which will be made available for a fee (usually a flat amount plus a per-unit charge) to customers. Both of these options serve to make EDP equipment more attractive to the small business. The first option makes it practical for many enterprises of intermediate size to rent or buy their own equipment. The second effectively eliminates a major problem by making it unnecessary for the small enterprise to have, by itself, a large enough volume of work to support the full cost of purchasing a computer or of renting the equipment for 40 hours a week.

EDP Program Development

There does remain a real problem, which is only partially resolved—the substantial cost of developing EDP programs appropriate for the particular enterprise. This is expensive and difficult and hard to justify where the volume of work is small. Some progress has been made through the development of standard, usually rather straightforward programs to carry out relatively standard specific functions—such as preparing payrolls—which occur in a large number of companies.   Additional progress has come from the development of more comprehensive, more complex programs to carry out more complex functions in more specific, rather highly defined, circumstances —e.g., in industries with a substantial number of essentially similar units, such as savings banks, savings and loan associations, automobile dealers, hospitals, and so on—for then the cost of program development can be widely shared. This is a particularly promising development where conditions make it practical. Where it is not practical (this is still the majority of cases), progress will probably be slower and more difficult because program packages which are not completely appropriate must be accepted, modified, or specially written for the single enterprise. Even in such instances, however, there is considerable promise, for functional packages can be and are being expanded, and the number of basic alternatives is being increased to provide the prospective user with at least more options, even if not with a program exactly appropriate for his enterprise. It can be concluded that comments about EDP made earlier have, with appropriate modifications, considerable relevance for the small enterprise and its management.

OPERATIONS RESEARCH

The second major new force—operations research—had its most significant roots in the military operations of World War II, when the skills and techniques of mathematicians and other scientists were enlisted to assist in and improve on the decision-making processes that previously had relied upon more intuitive means. Its successes far outranked its failures. No wonder that at the end of hostilities practitioners of operations research looked for new worlds to conquer and discerned, in the worlds of business and government, decisions and decision-making processes that had strong similarity to those to which they had grown accustomed.

Most observers would say that operations researchers have overcome the original reluctance of most business executives to admit (1) that such an occult art might have merit in business situations, and (2) that a somewhat arrogant, diverse group of men, with little or no knowledge of how the business world actually operates, should be the possessors of a talent useful to business. The reasons this reluctance has been overcome are not very complicated. The art is better understood; it no longer seems quite so occult. There are evidences of its results, which can be observed independently of the technique by which they were achieved. The original practitioners have acquired a knowledge of business and a vocabulary more like that which businessmen use; they have been joined by others whose education and experience is more directly oriented toward the problems of business. They have a somewhat more balanced view about the place of science and art in the management process.

As a useful oversimplification, it might be stated that the most valuable contributions of operations researchers have been their abilities (1) to use mathematical techniques in the solution of complex business problems, (2) to assist management in structuring these problems by defining and identifying their important elements more clearly and completely, and (3) to clarify and require that information be developed about costs and values and risks that had often not been developed in the past, or had not often been used in those councils where decisions were made.

Aims of Operations Research

Operations research, alternatively called "management science" or "mathematical management," is a discipline, skill, or body of knowledge and experience that believes that it is both possible and valuable to use the techniques and approaches of the scientific method in order to represent most business functions as mathematical models or formulas. It believes it is practical to obtain useful and realistic values for those formulas and to produce answers that will be helpful to executives in planning, in controlling, and, above all, in making decisions about their business. It relies heavily on probability, statistics, algebra, calculus, and other forms of mathematics. Its practitioners rely heavily on the investigations, analyses, and solution-testing approaches of the scientific method.

Typical Applications

A few examples will serve to indicate the kinds of things that operations research is trying to do. The most frequent, best "polished" applications of operations research lie in the field of inventory control. Managements have for generations known that the amount of inventory carried was the result of many different factors and pressures. The actual level was a compromise. It took into account a variety of factors such as how long it took to obtain the product, what the price was when different quantities were bought, whether there was a small or large or medium danger from obsolescence, how the customer would react if the company did not have the product in stock, and what storage costs would be. A fairly simple mathematical formula, often called the EOQ (Economic Order Quantity), was developed and fairly widely used. It took into account several of these factors—item cost, expected demand, ordering costs, and carrying costs.

The fundamental changes that the advent of management science has made in the field of inventory control have been (1) to incorporate a greater number of factors into the mathematical formulas, (2) to attempt to assign explicit values to factors that were formerly considered only in general terms, and (3) to give greater weight to the probability that certain events will or will not occur. Thus, the newer formulas include not only those items previously taken into account by the EOQ, but also the estimated frequency and cost of being out of stock, the concept of safety stock, and other factors. Values are assigned to factors (such as the cost of being out of stock) for which monetary values were not previously determined. By the use of probability and other sharper tools of measurement, costs and benefits are more correctly and precisely measured than in the past.

Other typical problems susceptible to the techniques of operations research can also be cited. Among the uses of these techniques are:

1. To determine the "best" method of distributing products from a number of factories through a number of warehouses to a number of customers.
2. To determine the "best" routes that traveling salesmen should take.
3. To predict the number of people required to issue stores from a storeroom, to act as tellers in a bank, or to collect tolls at a bridge in order to provide a desired standard of service under varying conditions.
4. To schedule the operation of a plant in order to balance the use of men, materials, and machinery and produce the "optimum" result.
5. To help in the establishment of "optimum" research and development or capital expenditure programs.
6. To simulate the impact of changes in plans or conditions on the operations of a division or a whole company.

In each of these cases, the essential contributions of management science are the formulas, the additional factors taken into account, the assignment of values to these factors, and the way probability is treated as a specific element of the decision.

The last three of these examples will be explored in some detail for they involve matters of greater complexity than are normally associated with inventory management. One should recognize that accomplishments to date vary in these areas, with the accomplishments tending to decrease as the size or complexity of the problem and the difficulty of predicting the future increase.

PLANT OPERATIONS SCHEDULING. Oil refinery operations and related decision factors can be expressed in mathematical terms; when so done, the resultant formulas will prove to be of substantial value in scheduling the refinery, arranging for crude oil purchases, and making other important operating decisions. These formulas have another use of great importance—they can more accurately predict the value of expenditures intended to add to or to modify the refinery itself. Capital expenditures that increase capacities, change processing techniques, or permit the use of different crudes or the production of different quantities of different products also result in new mathematical formulas that can be compared with the old. Economic and physical data resulting from this comparison can be useful to an executive wrestling with a capital investment decision, not only by producing a sounder decision but by providing a better documented basis for the prediction of future results.

RESEARCH AND DEVELOPMENT ALLOCATIONS. One of the most difficult decisions of a management that commits a substantial amount of money to research and development is to decide how much that total should be and how it should be allocated to individual projects. Any executive, regardless of whether mathematical techniques are employed, is pretty sure to consider probable cost, the chances of technical success, probable economic return, what might happen if competitors try and succeed and his company does not, whether the research project can be cut off at some intermediate point, other uses for the money, and so on. The process of reaching a decision is very difficult, particularly if there are a number of projects from which to choose. If one introduces the idea that there are various probabilities, it gets even more complicated—the odds may be 10 to 1 that the project will cost not more than $1,000,000; 2 to 1 that it will cost not more than $800,000; 1 to 20 that it might cost more than $1,500,000. As the decision gets more complicated, it also gets more realistic, for research costs are hard to estimate. If in considering what might happen if it decided *not* to proceed and competitors did go ahead and succeeded, a company merely said, "We would be hurt," that evaluation would be difficult to use very precisely in deciding what to do. If the company said, "We would be hurt to the extent of $100,000," or "The odds are 5 to 1 that we would be hurt to the extent of $100,000," information would have been produced that could be used much more readily in making a decision.

An executive seeking to choose from among a hundred research projects with varying probabilities, costs, and consequences would, it can be seen, find the methods and techniques of operations research—aided and abetted by the electronic computer—helpful in reaching a decision. In a way, management would be putting the calculation into what is now euphemistically and inaccurately referred to as the "calculated risk."

MATHEMATICAL MODELS. The last illustration, which involves the "company model," serves the purpose of further indicating the potential attraction of operations research for the business executive. It also underlines the greatest difficulty and weakness of that technique—the dependency of the methodology and the techniques upon the ability to analyze the past and predict the future in quantitative terms—in dollars or other measurable units.

There is no question that the development of an overall mathematical model showing how a company has acted and might be expected to act in the future in response to changes in internal and external forces would be of enormous value to management. The business executive could then determine what would probably happen in advance by the process of playing a serious "game" called "simulation." Through the introduction of different values for one or more of the factors that are part of the corporate model, the executive could see the probable effects on the company as a whole and on its parts. He could see what would be affected and by how much. He could see what might happen if other changes were made or if other events took place. He would have available in mathematical form for the purposes of experimentation, prediction, and the gaining of knowledge something not too dissimilar from the physical models that flood-control engineers use to study the behavior of rivers under varying water conditions. Mathematical simulation is a process that has already proved of value in such widely diversified activities as training aircraft pilots, designing bridges, scheduling oil refineries, and establishing inventory policy. It would be most valuable if it could make an equivalent contribution in other areas of business.

If a mathematical model could be constructed that was a faithful representation of reality, its value to overall corporate or division management would be enormous. If it did not represent reality, its value would be zero or negative. The value of simulation depends fundamentally on how good a job the model does of representing the situation as it is. Anyone acquainted with the problem of constructing a corporate model cannot fail to be impressed with the enormity of the problem involved; he also cannot fail to be excited by the possibilities if and when the size and impact of the various factors can be identified.

Impact on Managerial Information

The point of the foregoing examples is to indicate (1) that operations research is a new tool with great actual and potential value to the businessman, and (2) that it is a new and major force affecting both the nature and role of information in the managerial process. The information required is in many respects of the same type as that described earlier in this book. In many ways, however, it is different—more sophisticated, analyzed in more dynamic terms, more apt to be future-oriented. Even those companies with the most extensive and sophisticated information systems have found that they must rely on special studies and special analyses to gather the information they need. This is not a particularly satisfactory situation, for a number of reasons, but the chances are that it will exist for a long time to come.

Some companies have successfully altered information systems, particularly those that are heavily oriented toward machine-controlled manufacturing processes (a refinery, for example), but those examples are and will continue to be in a minority. The bigger effort will be to improve the development of needed information by means of the special study and the extension of quantitative information beyond past limits to the identification of values for risks, satisfactions, incremental costs and benefits, and rates of change.

EMPHASIS ON PLANNING AND THE
DECISION-MAKING PROCESS

The last of the major forces affecting the role of information in the managerial process did not enter the business scene of the last decade with either the suddenness or the radically innovative effects of computers or OR. Instead, it sprang from the heightened attention given to problems with which management had been concerned for many years. Business had long found it necessary to plan and to make decisions and had developed a concern as to how well it carried out its responsibilities. So had governmental units, and most particularly the military establishments. What happened to heighten the interest in planning and attendant decision making was that the amounts involved took a major jump in size, the risks involved frequently did the same, the number of alternative courses of action increased, and the time span required to carry out the plan and realize the results lengthened. It became increasingly apparent that once a plan was well under way, the opportunity to alter the course of action was severely limited. Three-, five-, and ten-year plans became an integral part of corporate life, of the military scene, and of the space program.

Impact of New Emphasis on Planning

Computers and the techniques of OR were enlisted in coping with this problem, but they were enlisted in support of other ideas not dependent upon new techniques or equipment. The first of the significant ideas resulting from the emphasis on planning has been a rather obvious one—to plan well on the new scale, for the new time period involved required a comparable increase in the quantity and quality of information available about the future. This meant that more attention had to be given to deciding what information should be obtained, who should get it, within what tolerances of accuracy it could and should be obtained, how much should be spent on gathering it, how the information should be presented and to whom, at what time and in what amount. Also, since much of the information was future-oriented—toward future needs of customers, future materials, future processes, future costs, future actions of competitors—the process of obtaining the information did not so much require clerks and statisticians to record and analyze known data as it did individuals with professional talents in economics, in markets, and in engineering technologies who could create as well as record information about what the future might hold. Thus, planning's increased emphasis made its first impact.

The second significant impact of the emphasis on planning has been the realization that if a sound choice is to be made there has to be (1) an identification of the various alternatives available and (2) a sound evaluation of the probable costs, risks, and consequences of each alternative. This has meant that more data have had to be obtained (especially the kind described in the discussion of operations research) to define and quantify costs, risks, and consequences in a way that makes the alternatives more susceptible to comparison. The evaluation of large projects, extending over the longer periods of the new planning cycle and often involving greater complexity and greater uncertainty, clearly is more difficult than when the time span was shorter and the possible actions were simple. It is not surprising, therefore, that planning has put new strains on the identification, estimating, and evaluation processes and has required that they be better organized, with staff qualifications superior to what had been required in the past.

Another impact of planning has been the realization that since on many occasions decisions have to be made about whole programs (rather than just about departments, products, or geographical areas) a way had to be found to accumulate and evaluate costs, risks, and consequences about whole programs rather than about their individual parts—products, departments, and areas.

Fourth, since some programs (e.g., social, welfare, or military-political) are related to intangible or only partially tangible results, techniques have had to be developed for accumulating information about and evaluating costs, risks, and consequences in areas that had previously been thought largely impervious to cost analysis, performance evaluation, and similar techniques.

The final impact has been the continued recognition that accumulations of costs and evaluations of results have to be related to the basis for planning—to keep the planners "honest"; to be able to modify, cancel, or continue existing plans within the limits permitted by those plans; to help decide upon future plans; to be able to hold the "doers" as well as the planners accountable for the attainment of results.

Planning, Programming, Budgeting System (PPBS)

One of the most striking and frequently discussed innovations has been the introduction of cost/effectiveness evaluation techniques into the Department of Defense and the restructuring of much of the Department's information system to provide more information about programs and program alternatives, costs, risks, consequences, and results. It is a rather striking illustration of the last three points made above.

The approach taken by the Department of Defense is the result of a vast change in outlook under which the Department elected to consider proposed and actual expenditures primarily in terms of their relative contribution to one or more of nine major strategic and tactical military programs and to almost 1,000 supporting "programmed elements." The Department thus broke with prior planning and control patterns which relied primarily on organizational responsibility and on a far smaller, less informative set of object categories (military personnel, R&D, transportation, construction, procurement, operations, and maintenance). The name given to the new approach, Planning, Programming, Budgeting System (PPBS), emphasizes that long-range planning of programs is to be encompassed within the framework of the budgeting system of the Department. The fact that actual expenditures and results are to be compared with budgeted programs makes the impact on the financial system complete.

Financial and non-financial executives alike have long recognized that ideally it would be desirable to be able to consider and record proposed and actual expenditures from four points of view. They have also recognized that the difficulty of doing this increases sharply as one moves down the following list:

1. The nature of expenditure—i.e., manpower, materials, etc.
2. The organizational responsibility.
3. The purpose of the expenditure in terms of the organizational unit making the expenditure.
4. The purpose of the expenditure in terms of the enterprise as a whole.

PPBS attempts to shift the emphasis heavily toward the fourth classification on the assumption that it is essential to planning and control in terms of the overall objectives of the military establishment. This creates many problems of interpretation and many difficult technical accounting and statistical problems of identification and allocation. This explains both why PPBS is a major and somewhat imperfect system and why this idea—planning and budgeting by program—is a force having a major impact on the whole of the information process.

The space program, for example, draws heavily upon the ideas and techniques of PPBS. The techniques of PPBS—with antecedents both within and without the Department of Defense—have also been introduced into many of the other departments and agencies of the federal government, with strong backing from the Bureau of the Budget and from the President. By example or request, similar systems are beginning to appear on an increasingly widespread basis at state, county, and local levels. They are beginning to appear in non-governmental institutions, particularly those with non-profit objectives. Ultimately, they will appear in some form in industrial enterprises as a technique for dealing more effectively with expenditures not directly related to the manufacture of the product.

Many of the governmental programs—particularly those with social, welfare, educational, research, and similar aims—have objectives that are often hard to define in other than intangible terms, with results that are even more difficult to measure. One can state and measure the number of hours of social-worker time with relative ease; stating the objectives of and probable results of that time in terms of a proposed program which must be evaluated against other programs, and then subsequently recording and measuring the results obtained is another matter. It is evident, however, that as the governmental and non-governmental institutions and industry continue their efforts to define and evaluate essentially intangible programs, a great deal of useful knowledge will be gained which will further enhance the value of the PPBS idea in such areas. It is quite conceivable that industry will find great value in planning and controlling research, advertising, and many other types of overhead costs on the basis of ideas developed in this manner.

Other techniques could be cited—e.g., PERT, PERT/COST, CPM—to support the point already made. The greater emphasis on planning and subsequently controlling and evaluating plans and performance has become and will continue to be one of the major forces affecting both the nature and the role of information in the managerial process.

DUAL ROLE OF INFORMATION

It can be seen quite clearly that the role of information in the managerial process is both supportive and creative. It supports the executive—in large or small businesses, in government, or in institutional enterprises—in planning, operating, and controlling the enterprise by the use of a variety of managerial techniques. Information technology is also creative, however, since the ability to make new types of information available within new time spans to different parts of the organization permits the executive not only to improve on old management methods but to create new techniques for planning, operating, and controlling the business.

In a period in which great changes are taking place in the tools of data processing, in ideas about how to analyze and present information in the most useful manner, and in the needs of managers for information, it is logical to find that both the supportive and the creative aspects of information are deeply affected.

9

Evaluating a Management Information System

If the basic purpose of this book has been accomplished, it has been demonstrated, both in theory and by example, that information can play an important role in supporting the efforts of managers. It also should have been made evident that information systems vary greatly in their effectiveness, falling all along the scale from poor to excellent in providing this support.

There are several ways of determining where, within this scale, a particular information system falls—where its strengths and its deficiencies lie. Taking one approach, an executive can compare what his company is doing with what "advanced companies" have found to be desirable; almost always he will discover that improvements can be made. Beyond such a comparison, however, if an executive possesses the requisite skill and experience, he can take the measure of both the quantity and quality of information provided in a specific enterprise in terms of (1) a set of general criteria and (2) the specific needs of the particular management. Some of what is involved in the latter evaluation is the subject matter of this chapter.

The approach taken in evaluating an information system, more often than not, will be twofold:

1. To look for indications of the adequacy and inadequacy of the information system as mirrored in the attitudes, actions, and working habits of the executives comprising management.

2. To look at the adequacy or inadequacy of the management information system itself—its content, its sources, its method of presentation.

SYMPTOMS OF INADEQUATE INFORMATION

Symptoms of inadequate management information are often not too hard to find. They vary from the essentially emotional or psychological to those reflected in the executives' styles of management to those caused more directly by the substance of the information itself. The following symptoms are typical:

1. An approach to management that makes profuse use of hunches in the process of making decisions, even when facts are available.
2. An absence of effective planning and control.
3. A surplus of knowledge about internal matters, accompanied by a relatively shallow awareness of conditions in the "outside world."
4. A lack of understanding of financial terms and information among the non-financial members of the executive group.
5. Lots of managerial surprises—physical inventory adjustments, imbalances in orders and production, capital expenditure overruns.
6. Unexplainable differences from plans, expectations, and standards—profit variations, cost changes, order drop-offs.
7. Complaints about errors, lateness, "perfectionitis," excessive detail, conflicting data.

While some problems and symptoms are normal and to be expected, when they appear in excessive number or with excessive severity there is almost certainly something wrong. But the fault is not necessarily with the information system, for some or all of the problems can often be attributed to other causes—poor organization, inadequate personnel, and improper managerial methods, to name a few. Even where the symptoms indicate that the probable cause of failure lies in the information system, it is wise to confirm this by a direct examination of the information system itself.

INSPECTION OF THE INFORMATION SYSTEM

What does a person evaluating an information system seek to discover? What questions does he try to answer? The topics discussed in the following sections are probably the most important.

Matching Information Generated Against Management Responsibilities

Does the information fit in well with the responsibilities of management? Does it satisfy the needs of the management process?

Management interest in information is largely utilitarian and pragmatic. Will the information help in carrying out the functions management is called upon to perform? Will it, more specifically, help in reaching the decisions and taking the actions that are their responsibility—in planning, organizing, executing, and controlling operations and in the successive recycling of the management process as replanning, reorganizing, reexecuting, and recontrolling occur on the basis of the feedback of results?

Whether the information provided performs this function satisfactorily or not depends, in the last analysis, upon its relevance to management's problems and management's willingness and ability to use it. Information will be most relevant when it (1) contributes to the key decisions that must be made and (2) focuses on the key success factors for a particular company at a particular stage of its development. Relevance to key decisions and key factors implies that the same information will have different values to different companies in different industries and even to the same company at different times. The logical conclusion, therefore, is that while some information will be found to be more important more often than other information, there is no cookbook or stereotyped list of what should be furnished. The evaluator's first task is to determine relevance.

Scope and Balance of Information

Does the information system embody a broad view of what information is, or is the orientation excessively narrow?

There is a limited yet widely held view which, unconsciously or not, seems to contend that information is essentially internal (about the company itself), historical (about the past), or financial. It is not that other types of information—external, present- and future-oriented, and non-financial—do not exist; but there is a severe imbalance in favor of the former stemming from its availability, its accuracy, and its other advantages. A much more rational distribution of effort exists, especially in terms of relevance to managerial decisions and problems, when more of the time and money spent on developing and producing information recognizes this fact. Data about customers, competitors, economic conditions, impending technological and market-oriented developments, for example, may be less available and less precise but very significant. Figures on estimated future costs or order positions may be of equal or greater importance than similar information about the past. Data on problems of quality, employee turnover, etc., will normally be clearer and more readily available in quantitative (non-dollarized) terms.

The checklist on pages 139–141 setting forth the major information requirements of a manufacturing company indicates that the needs for information are many and varied. The need for a balanced and broad point of view seems clear. An examination to see that there is a proper balance of data is one of the requirements of an evaluation survey.

Informal Collection and Reporting Methods

Does the information system make use of the various means of communication available to it or is its approach excessively formal?

An excessive reliance on formality can sharply reduce the value of information; informality should be accorded its legitimate place. Most companies, particularly those of more than minimal size, will rely primarily on formal methods for collecting, recording, summarizing, and presenting information. This approach will be taken because (1) the volume of data requires it, (2) there is inadequate assurance that an unassigned or informally assigned responsibility will be discharged, (3) the recipients (and users) of the information are often not available at a common time or not located at a common place, and (4) much of the information will be useful if available for study over a longer period of time than one's memory can sustain. There is really no quarrel with formality in its place.

Excessive reliance on the formal collection of data can, however, prove to be a handicap, for much information—e.g., about markets and customers and products—is discovered, by using informal methods which should not require rediscovery by formal techniques. Once obtained, there should be opportunity for it to reach the individuals who are in a position to use it.

Excessive reliance on formality can also harm the transmission of data to the user. It can slow up the process (by requirements for excessive accuracy, or "pretty" reports) so that it arrives too late to be of maximal value. It can also confuse the process by failing to provide for discussions that will highlight significant matters, clear up misunderstandings, and make sure that all parties see the situation in the same light.

The evaluator has many ways of approaching this question. He can look at the types and numbers of opportunities that executives provide for obtaining information from informal sources—visits, discussions, meetings, etc. He can see how or whether informally gathered information flows from subordinates to superiors. He can investigate the nature and extent of reliance on inter-executive committees or on similar top departmental groups. He can see the extent to which formal reports are forced to speak for themselves without the benefit of oral presentation and discussion. He can see to what extent drama and excitement are introduced (by "corny" means or otherwise) into the information process.

Bases of Data Comparison

Does the information system use appropriate bases of comparison?

The difficulties of properly understanding and appropriately using naked data soon lead most users of information to insist upon the introduction of one or more bases of comparison. The selection of the most appropriate basis or bases is the first half or perhaps the first quarter of the problem. The remainder is whether the comparative data actually provide the kind of basis for comparison that the user of the information believes they do, and therefore whether or not the actual comparison made by him is valid.

A comparison of this year's and last year's results has both values and limitations which are usually sufficiently obvious for the risk of misunderstanding to be minimized—not too much is promised and not too much is expected. As one moves toward budgets and standards and the user's expectations rise, the validity of the data contained in the comparative base assumes a greater degree of significance. One experienced with information systems comes to expect that the validity of the base's data will vary enormously. An evaluation of a specific system must therefore take this fact into account.

Form of Data Presentation

Is the form of presentation appropriate?

For information to have value it must be used. To be used it must be conveyed: it must be heard or seen, and understood by the individual executive in a way that has meaning. The form and method of presenting information to management bears importantly upon whether it will be understood and used. Several alternative forms of possible presentation (alone or in combination) are listed below:

1. Written—tabulations of figures, charts or graphs, narratives, in-depth analyses.
2. Oral—scheduled presentations, chart-room discussions, face-to-face reports, telephone or audio inquiry devices.
3. Visual—personal inspection, and visual display devices.

In some situations, written reports are best suited for conveying information, making it understood, and obtaining a reaction. The particular form of written report that is most useful depends upon the purposes of the particular information. Narrative reports, for example, are useful for conveying qualitative information that is difficult to quantify. Bar charts or pie charts are frequently more useful than tabulations of figures where comparative relationships are important.

In many situations, oral and visual presentations are a vastly superior way of informing the executive. For example, chart rooms often offer an opportunity to transmit information to a number of individuals simultaneously. This technique enables executives, while the ideas are still fresh, to voice and exchange opinions, to arrive at a common understanding, and often to take action on the spot. Oral and visual presentations help to insure understanding; they force consideration of the facts in a way that written reports do not. As does advertising, they make motivation easier than do written reports.

To a certain extent the techniques used to present information must fit into the pattern of communications that the company generally employs. Of course, information can break with that pattern or even help to start another, if that is appropriate. An individual appraising an information system finds it helpful to consider this carefully.

Management's Capacity To Use Information

Does the information system take into account management's capacity to use information?

The great variations in management's ability to use information properly in running a business are based on a variety of factors—education, training, occupational experience, the size and complexity of the enterprise, among others. As a consequence, it is quite possible to overproduce or to underproduce information for management, as well as to match information with management's needs in the same situation. There is a minimum and a maximum beyond which a management should not go, and it would seem to be the responsibility of management and of the "information producers" to seek to establish those limits. Between those two points, however, will normally be found a range within which a choice can be made reflecting the capabilities, desires, and managerial philosophy of the management group.

One can make the unqualified statements (1) that the newer executives and the younger managers have for at least the past decade shown expanded capabilities for using information and (2) that the executives of the future, reflecting in part the needs of their businesses and in part the orientation of their business education, will probably be pushing hard on those who supply information, rather than the reverse.

No matter what a company's general or overall levels of ability to use information, now or at some future date, there will always be inequalities with which to contend. Information is usually produced only at an economic cost; its economic value will vary with the characteristics of management, and some allowance must be made for that fact.

The appraisal of information can be seen to require (1) that certain qualitative judgments of the type just described be made and (2) that the evaluations thus made be compared with the reactions indicated by management. The final determination should indicate where the strengths and weaknesses lie and the nature of the corrective program that is appropriate for the specific company in its specific circumstances.

Major Information Requirements
of a Manufacturing Company

- **FACILITIES AND METHODS**

  Physical Characteristics of Existing Facilities

  Capacity and Utilization

  Technological Status

  Deficiencies and Opportunities
  - Quality problems
  - Production inefficiency
  - Imbalances in productive facilities

  Capital Expenditure Opportunities and Requests

  Capital Expenditures
  - Control of in-progress projects
  - Follow-up for results

  Maintenance Problems and Costs

  Work Methods
  - Results of past improvements
  - Potential improvements

- **PRODUCTS**

  What Product Line Is

  Stage in Growth/Decline Cycle—Trends

  Extent of Coverage Provided

  Competitive Product Evaluation
  - Direct
  - Substitutes

  Quality vs. Specifications

  Performance in Terms of Customer Needs

  New Products or Product Improvements

  Profitability

  Reactions to Products
  - Customers
  - Salesmen

  Guaranty/Warranty Situation

  Cost/Value Information Relative to Product Design

- **MANUFACTURING COSTS**

  Present and Historical Costs for
  - Products
  - Components, packaging
  - Departments
  - Processes
  - Cost categories

  Standards and Deviations
  - Tightness of standards
  - Cause and trend of deviations

  Direct-Period-Programed Costs

  Make/Buy Study Results

  Labor Productivity
  - Direct and indirect
  - Overtime and extra costs

  Quality Reject and Rework Costs

  Idle or Unused Capacity Costs

  Economic Lot Sizes—Manufacturing

  Cost Reduction Effort Results

- **PHYSICAL PRODUCTION PLANNING AND INVENTORIES**

  Sales Order Position

  Purchase Order Position

  Economic Lot Size — Purchasing — and Purchasing Points

  Vendor Performance

  Production Schedule

  Production Cycle Lead-Time

  Machine Loading and Labor Schedule

  Inventory Positions, Including Turnover

Major Information Requirements—Continued

• PRICES

Price Structure

    Ours

    Competitors'

Price Deviations

Relationship of Volume Changes to Changes in Price, Quality and Other Interrelated Factors

• MARKETING AND DISTRIBUTION

Marketing and Distribution Methods Employed and Their Effectiveness

    Ours

    Competitors'

Marketing Support and Its Effectiveness

    Advertising and promotion

    Technical service

Adequacy of Customer Service, Including Delivery Performance

    Ours

    Competitors'

Effectiveness of Salesmen

Sales Performance

    Vs. forecast/budget

    Incoming orders

    New account analysis

    Lost account analysis

    Lost orders analysis

    Return sales analysis

    Customer complaint analysis

Profitability by

    Type of distribution

    Type of customer

    Geographical area

Marketing and Distribution Expense Control

"Health" of Dealer Organization

Customer Inventory Situation

Reciprocal Sales

• RESEARCH AND DEVELOPMENT

Knowledge of Research Discoveries and Advances in Existing Knowledge

Research Opportunities

Research Goals and Balance of Effort

Research Proposal Evaluation

    Product improvements

    New products

    New materials

    Process improvements

Research Projects

    Status—technical

    Status—cost

Research Personnel

    Qualifications

    Experience

Scientist Support

Historical Evidence of Value of Research to Company

• EMPLOYEES

Organization Structure, Duties, and Responsibilities

Management

    Appraisals

    Incumbent situation — continuity and succession

    Compensation and benefits

Work Force

    Numbers

    Turnover

    Skills and age distribution

    Compensation and benefits

    Morale and attitude

    Union grievances

    Separation analysis

    Shortages ("open to hire")

    Availability

Employee Suggestions

Major Information Requirements—Continued

- **FINANCIAL**

  Cash and Working Capital Positions, Forecasts, Analyses

  Current Ratios

  Line of Credit Utilization

  Temporary Investment Opportunities

  Accounts Receivable Turnover, Age, Collection Status, Problem Accounts

  Inventory Investment Analysis

  Debt to Equity Status

  Adequacy of Reserves

  Analysis of Surplus

  Long-Term Spending Requirements

  Sources and Availability of Capital

  Short-Term Requirements

  Money Market Developments

  Stock

    Ownership changes

    Prices and P/E trends

    Analyst opinions

  Lease Obligations

  Financial Guarantees and Other Contingent Obligations

  Adequacy of Insurance Coverage

  Tax Situation

  Internal Accounting Control Situation

- **MARKETS**

  Share of Market

    Ours

    Competitors'

  Size of Total Market

  Forces Determining Size and Nature of Market

  Sales Forecasts

- **GENERAL**

  Basic B/S and P/L and Cash-Flow Information

    Ours

    Competitors'

  Return on Investment

  Break-Even Points

  Budgets and Long-Range Plans

  Variations from Budgets and Plans and Standards

  External Factors

    Economic conditions

    Political

    Labor situation, tax situation, etc.

  Corporate Objectives

  Community–Company Relationships

Glossary of Business and Information Terms

Accounting—The art or system of recording the transactions entered into by an enterprise and of so classifying and analyzing them that significant financial and statistical data will be revealed.

Accounting, accrual—The system of accounting that (1) records transactions as assets and liabilities when obligations are incurred rather than when cash is paid or received, and (2) assigns income and expenses to the period to which they are related rather than to the period in which they are settled in cash. Another system of accounting—cash accounting—records assets and liabilities, income and expenses when the receipt or payment of cash takes place.

Accounting, cost—That portion of the accounting system primarily concerned with determining how much it "costs" to make a product, to carry out an operation, to perform a service, etc. While usually thought of in relation to manufacturing, it can also be applied to determine research, distribution, and other non-manufacturing costs.

Asset, fixed—An asset such as land, buildings, or equipment—not intended to be converted into cash within the next year—whose value to the company will extend over a longer period of time.

Assets, intangible—Goodwill, patent, organization, and similar costs, essentially non-physical in nature, which are often considered to have less than fully demonstrable value to an enterprise.

Balance sheet—A statement showing assets, liabilities, and shareholders' equity on a specific date.

Bill of materials—A list of the materials, parts, and assemblies or subassemblies, and the quantity of each, required to make a product or to build the items specified by a particular order.

Break-even chart—A chart showing the relationships of costs, prices, volumes, and profits under varying conditions; it gets its name

143

from the fact that the point where neither a profit nor loss will be earned is clearly indicated.

Burden—Manufacturing expenses other than direct materials and labor incurred in manufacturing a product, rendering a service, etc.; often called overhead or indirect costs.

Carrying costs—The expenses incurred in acquiring and maintaining a level of inventory.

Cash flow—Net income after adding back expense items which currently do not use funds, such as depreciation. It may also involve deducting revenue items which do not currently provide funds, such as the current amortization of deferred income.

Channel of distribution—The method or type of organization through which a product moves from the manufacturer to the ultimate customer. Direct mail, wholesale, retail stores, department stores, sales force, jobber, and agent are involved in typical channels.

Cost—The expenditures made to produce a product, perform a function, or render a service.

Cost, marginal—The additional cost required to make an additional unit of product.

Cost, variable—A cost which changes as the volume of business changes.

Costs, direct—Costs which can be directly identified with a specific product or lot of production; e.g., the wage of a machine operator who works on a specific product is a direct cost of that product.

Costs, indirect—Costs which cannot be directly identified with a specific product or lot of production, such as the rent of a factory in which more than one product is manufactured.

Depreciation—The charge made to profit and loss for the use of fixed assets such as buildings, machinery and equipment, or cars and trucks. The charge is intended to allocate the cost (less estimated salvage value) of these assets to expense over a period of years. The charge made in a single year reflects not only the estimated total life of the asset but also the method of depreciation used. Straight-line depreciation spreads the cost of the asset equally over the years; double-declining-balance, sum-of-the-year's-digits, and other methods accelerate depreciation by making larger charges in the earlier years.

Earnings—The net profits or net income of an enterprise; that which remains after all expenses are deducted from sales. At times, the term "earnings" is used to describe something other than *net* income but the unqualified term (as in "earnings per share") usually means net income.

Expense—An expenditure made in the current or another period which is charged against income in the current accounting period.

FIFO—An abbreviation of the phrase "first-in, first-out." A method of pricing inventory in which prices are identified with quantities received and it is assumed that those quantities received first are also sold or used first and that the inventory remaining on hand came from the most recent receipts. (See LIFO for a contrasting method.)

Financial position—The status of a company on a specific date as demonstrated by its balance sheet.

Fiscal period—A length of time, usually a month or a year, for which the enterprise prepares statements showing its financial position and earnings.

Gross national product—The nation's output of goods and services during the period of a year, expressed in dollars.

Gross profit—The result of subtracting the cost of goods sold from sales or revenue received. It is called gross profit (as distinguished from net profit) because other business expenses have not yet been deducted.

Income, net—The profit resulting after all costs and expenses—cost of goods sold; selling, general, and administrative expenses; income taxes, etc.—have been deducted from sales.

Indirect labor—Labor not specifically identified with those operations which directly make the product.

Internal control—Measures taken within the enterprise to protect assets from improper use or theft and to assure the accuracy of financial and other data. Strong reliance is placed on proper authorization and approval, a division of duties, and a system of checks and balances.

Inventory—Materials, supplies, parts, and finished products which are in storage or in process, awaiting use or sale.

Inventory turnover—The number of times that an item or group of items is sold or used in a given period, usually a year. This ratio can also be computed by dividing the cost of the inventory into the cost of the items used or sold in the period.

Job shop—A company which makes products or does work "to order" according to its customers' specifications.

LIFO—An abbreviation of the phrase "last-in, first-out"; the opposite of FIFO. A method of pricing inventory in which prices are identified with quantities received and it is assumed that the quantities received last are sold or used first.

Marginal income—The amount which the sale of an additional unit adds to total income.

Market research—The testing and investigation carried on in connection with the product and the marketing function in such areas as product characteristics, packaging, pricing, the distribution system, the kind of person the consumer is, probable demand, and competitive position.

Net loss—The excess of all costs and expenses—cost of goods sold; selling, general, and administrative expenses; income taxes, etc.—over sales and other income.

Net profit—The excess of sales and other income over costs and expenses, including income taxes.

Net worth—The shareholders' equity in a business as represented by the excess of total assets over total liabilities; in a corporation, the shareholders' equity is the total of the capital stock and surplus.

Obsolescence—The condition or process by which assets cease to be useful or profitable because of economic, social, or technological changes.

Organization chart—A graphic representation of the structure of a business firm, showing the various organizational units and the lines of responsibility governing their interrelationships.

Overhead—Manufacturing expenses other than direct materials and labor incurred in manufacturing a product or rendering a service.

Product analysis—A study of products to develop new ones, adapt old ones to new uses, or determine product characteristics most valuable to the consumer. Also, the study of how to provide the greatest value per dollar of cost or sales price.

Production control—The scheduling and controlling of the use of men, materials, and machinery in order to produce goods on time and in an efficient manner.

Profit and loss statement—A detailed statement showing revenue less the cost of goods sold and other expenses with the resulting net profit or loss for a specified period. Also known as an income statement.

Quality control—A system, based in part on inspection, which is used to assure the uniform and acceptable compliance of a product with its specifications.

Ratio, current—The ratio of current assets to current liabilities. This is sometimes called "the bankers' ratio" because bankers commonly use it in credit analysis.

Return on investment—The ratio of net income from the business as a whole, from a part of it, or from a specific capital expenditure to the assets or investment on which it was earned.

Revenue—The gross amount charged to customers for goods and services.

Sales forecast—An estimate of dollar or unit sales for a future period.

Standardization—The act of establishing and maintaining specific production criteria for materials, weights, measurements, wearability, and serviceability. Also, the act of limiting parts used to a prespecified list.

Statement of account—A monthly itemized statement sent to a credit customer of a business.

Surplus—The amount by which the assets exceed the liabilities and capital stock of a company. It has little or no direct relationship to the amount of cash on hand.

Variance—A deviation from a standard or forecast.

Index

Accountants, 59
Accounting, 143
    accrual, 143
    cost, 143
Accounts receivable, 8
    collections from customers, 91–92, 96
    to compare current results, 16
    compared with sales, 12
    follow-up system for collection, 97–98
Accuracy of information and data, 8
Administration, inventory management and, 82–83
Advertising agencies
    market research, 59
    obtaining information from, 58–59
Advertising programs, 36, 43, 54
    costs, 42
Alternative choices, 24–29
    cost and profit analyses; see Cost and profit analyses
    costs, risks, and consequences, 127–28
    evaluation, 51
    identification of, 127
    risks involved, 126
Assets
    comparisons of current liabilities and, 12
    fixed, 143
    intangible, 143
Authority, delegation of, 101–10

Bad debt losses, 91
Balance sheets, 34, 143, 145
    projections, 25
Banks and banking, 59
    financing by, 93–94
    information required, 99–100
Bill of materials, 73, 143
Billing procedures, 97
    invoices, 97

Break-even charts, 38, 40, 44, 143–44
Budgets and budgeting, 25
    capital expenditure, 28–29
    cash, 28–29, 94–95
        comparing plan and results, 94–95
        estimating receipts, 91–94
        lag between outlays and receipts, 88–91
        period for, 87–88
        seasonal changes, 87, 90
    continuing process, 25–28
    control, 49, 109
    flow chart, 25–26
    information required, 29–30
    long-range, 25
    measures of performance, 109
    operating, 26, 28
    Planning, Programming, Budgeting System (PPBS), 128–30
    review and revision, 27–29
Building trade, 15
Burden, 144

Capital expenditures
    approval program, 109
    budgeting, 28–29
    cash management and, 86–87, 89
    effect of cost, price, and profit information on, 50
    planning, 28–29
    use of operations research, 123
Cash management, 67, 84–100
    bad debt losses, 91
    bank financing, 93–94, 99–100
    billing procedures, 97
    budgeting, 25, 26, 94–95
        comparing performance and plan, 94–95
        period of, 87–88
        seasonal changes, 87, 90
    cash balances, 9

Cash management (*Continued*)
  cash flow, 88–91, 144
    lag between outlays and receipt of cash, 89
    projections, 25
  cash forecasts, 86
  comparing actual performance and plan, 94–95
  corporate policies, 93–94
  credit policy, 96–97
  determining requirements, 86–87
  estimating cash receipts, 91–94
    collections from customers, 91–92
    financing from outside sources, 92–94, 98–100
  follow-up system, 97–98
  information for planning, 95–100
  internal generation of cash, 96–98
  investing excess funds, 98
  key problems in, 85–94
  lag between outlays and receipts, 88–91
  long- and short-term loans, 92–94
  ratio to current liabilities, 16
  securing cash from outside sources, 98–100
  working capital, 93–94
Catalogs
  parts and materials, 73–74
  substitution or alternate list, 74
Channel of distribution, 144
Charts and graphs, 10, 11, 136–37
Collections, from customers, 91–92
Comparisons
  bases for comparing current results, 11–18
  competitive, 14–16
  past or historical, 12–13
  periods and trends, 13
  planned, 13–14
  present or current, 11–12
  reliability and accuracy, 12–13
  selection of appropriate periods for, 13
  true potential, 14
Competition, 56
  bases for comparing current results, 14–16
  marketing and product information, 62
  obtaining information about, 53–54
  sources of information about, 53–57

Computers, 111–19
  accessibility of information, 117
  analysis and summarization of records, 115
  applications, 119
  communication equipment used with, 111–19
  coordination of interdepartmental activities, 114
  cost and accuracy of information, 112–13
  cost of developing programs, 119
  customer credit status, 116
  "data banks," 117
  EDP program development, 119
  effect on centralized or decentralized organization, 115–17
  effect on decision-making, 115–17
  extension and supervision of delegated authority, 115
  impact of data processing, 111–12
  inventory information, 116
  manufacturing capacity, 116
  new ideas and techniques, 112
  program packages, 119
  rent or purchase of, 118–19
  risks involved in developing, 118
  service centers, 118
  short-term planning and control, 113
  small business use of, 118
  speed of information availability, 113–14
  use of, 56
Consultants, 59, 63
Conventions, trade
  competitive information, 61
Cost and profit analyses
  analysis of profit by line of business, 36–38
  analyzing company by line of business, 34–36
  analyzing company by variability of costs, 36–38
  break-even charts, 38, 40, 44
  gross profit on certain models, 41
  predictions under varying conditions, 44–47
  profit variances with volume, 38–39
  sales and cost classifications, 47–48
  special, 34–38
  types of useful reports, 47
  using, 38–47

Cost/effectiveness evaluation techniques, 128–30
Costs
  advertising, 42
  capacity, 43
  carrying, 75, 144
  classifications of, 47–48
  committed, 37, 42–44, 46
  definition, 144
  direct, 144
  direct labor, 42
  direct materials, 42
  indirect, 144
  long-term actions, 36
  "managed," 42–43
  manufacturing, 34
  marginal, 144
  overhead, 36, 42
  prices, profits, and, 31–51
    benefits of information, 48–51
    declining-profit problem, 31–34
    plans based on, 48–49
    profit predictions under varying conditions, 44–47
    reports, 47–48
    special cost and profit analyses, 34–38
    using cost and profit analyses, 38–47
    variable, committed, and programmed costs, 42–44
  programmed, 37, 42–44
  sales commissions, 42, 46
  selling expenses, 34
  special cost and profit analyses, 34–38
  unit, 43
  unit production, 5
  variable, 36–38, 42–44, 144
CPM techniques, 130
Credit policies, 56, 96–97
  collections from customers, 91–92, 96
Customers
  collections from, 91–92
  credit status, 116
  industrial, 63–64
  negotiations with, 49–50
  obtaining information from, 60–61, 63
  reactions, 56–57
  as source of information, 53, 56

statement of account, 147
technical assistance for, 65

Data
  bases of comparisons, 11–18, 135–36
  presentation of, 136–37
  reliability, 8
  significance and vitality, 7–8
  timeliness, 9–10
  understandability, 10–11
Dealers and distributors, as source of information, 58, 63
Decision-making
  effect of computers on, 115–17
  emphasis on, 126–30
  operations research technique, 120–25
Defense Department, use of Planning, Programming, Budgeting System (PPBS), 128–30
Delegation of authority, 101–10
  amount of authority, 104
  basic approaches, 104–05
  chain of command, 108–09
  computers aid in extension and supervision of, 115
  control and, 101–10
    degree of control, 104–05
  freedom to manage, 109–10
  information required, 105–08
    company policies, 105
    results expected, 105–06
    limitations imposed, 106–08
  necessity for, 102–03
  reluctance to, 103–04
  responsibilities, 101–04
  reviewing results, 109
  specific area of, 104
Delivery dates, 74, 80
Depreciation, 43, 144
Direct labor costs, 42
Direct materials costs, 42
Distribution, channel of, 144
Distribution policies, 50–51

Earnings, 144–45
Electronic data processing (EDP), 111–19
  accessibility of information to decision makers, 117
  computers and, 111–19; see also Computers

Electronic data processing (EDP) (*Continued*)
coordination of interdepartmental activities, 114–15
cost and accuracy of information, 112–13
extension and supervision of delegated authority, 115
opportunity to centralize and decentralize, 115–17
program development, 119
short-term planning and control, 113
speed of information availability, 113–14
Employees, as source of market information, 56
Estimates or approximations, 9
Estimates of future demands, 69–72
Evaluation of information system, 131–38
bases of data comparison, 135–36
charts and graphs, 136–37
collection and reporting methods, 134–35
inspection of, 133–38
management's capacity to use, 137–38
marketing and product information, 64–66
presentation of data, 136–37
relevance to management's responsibilities, 133
scope and balance, 134
symptoms of inadequate information, 132
Executives; *see* Management
Expenses, definition, 145

Federal Trade Commission
The Quarterly Financial Report of Manufacturing Corporations, 15
Feedback, use of, 5
Financial position, 145
Finished goods, 68
Fiscal period, 145
Flow chart, corporate planning, 25
Follow-up system, 97–98
Forecasts, 70–71
cash, 86
estimates of future demand, 69–72
orders on hand, 71–72
revisions, 25–27, 71

Fourteen Important Ratios (Dun & Bradstreet), 15
Future trends, information on, 126–27

Glossary of business and information terms, 143–47
Government publications, marketing information in, 62
Governmental units
emphasis on planning, 126–30
use of PPBS techniques, 128
Gross national product, definition, 145
Gross profit, 145
comparing information, 17

Housing starts, 15–16

Income
marginal, 146
net, 145
Indirect labor, 145
Industry associations, information available from, 15
Information on current results, 3–18
to answer "how we stand," 5–6
approach to, 18
bases for comparing, 11–18
competitive, 14–16
past or historic, 12–13
periods selected, 13
planned, 13–14
present or current, 11–12
true potential, 14
incentive for making better plans, 5–6
to indicate trouble spots, 5
internal sources, 56–57
kinds of, 16–17
markets and product, 55–62
company records, 57
employees, 56–57
internal sources, 56–57
organizing, 6–7
for planning decisions, 5
purpose of, 4–6
requirements of good, 6–18
bases for comparing, 11–18
reliability, 8–9
significance and vitality of, 7–8
timeliness, 9–10
understandability, 10–11
as stimulus to action, 5–6
supportive and creative, 130

systems, 125; *see also* Information systems
use of, 4–6
Information systems
bases of data comparison, 135–36
charts and graphs, 136–37
collection and reporting methods, 134–35
dual role of information, 130
evaluating, 131–38
form of data presentation, 136–37
information requirements of manufacturing companies, 134, 139–41
inspection of, 133–38
management's capacity to use, 137–38
relevance to management responsibilities, 133
scope and balance of, 134
symptoms of inadequate information, 132
Insurance, 43
Internal control, 145
Internal sources of information, 56–57
Inventories
analysis of records, 56
bill of materials, 73, 143
carrying costs, 77–78
cash invested in, 77
comparisons, 16
with unfilled orders, 12
condition of, 77–78
control
application of operations research, 121–22
EOQ (Economic Order Quantity), 121–22
obsolescence, 121
cost of being out of stock, 122
definition, 145
effect on administration, 82–83
effect on costs, 68
effect on manufacturing activities, 78–79
effect on operating performance, 76–83
effect on purchasing, 79–81
effect on sales, 81–82
estimates of future demands, 69–72
forecasts, 70–71
orders on hand, 71–72
FIFO method, 145
finished goods, 68

function of, 67–68
information most useful in managing, 68–76
investments in, 96
levels, 75–78
factors favoring large, 76
factors favoring small, 76
relative value of different, 75–76
LIFO, 145–46
management of, 67–68
part and material specifications, 73–74
catalogs and parts list, 73–74
periodic status reports, 75
physical examination of, 68
predicting requirements, 79
production schedules, 74
purchased parts, 68, 74
raw materials, 68, 70, 74
records, 68
standardization of items, 77, 80
storage costs, 121
turnover ratios, 12, 145
use of computers, 116
work in progress, 68, 74
Investments
excess funds, 98
profitability of proposed, 29
return on, 147

Job shop, 145

Labor
direct labor costs, 42
indirect, 145

Magazines, source of marketing information, 61
Management
capacity to use information, 137–38
delegation and control, 101–10
amount of authority, 104
area for, 104
basic approaches, 104–05
degree of control, 104–05
information required, 105–08
limitations on, 106–08
reluctance for, 103–04
reviewing results, 109–10
emphasis on planning and decision-making process, 126–30
inventory management and, 82–83

Management (*Continued*)
  operations research, 120–25
  role of information, new forces affecting, 111–30
  dual role, 130
Management science, 121; *see also* Operations research
Manufacturing, effect of inventories on, 78–79
Manufacturing companies, information requirements, 134, 139–41
Manufacturing data, comparing information, 17
Margin of error, 8
Marginal income, 146
Market and product information
  from accountants, bankers, and consultants, 59
  advertising agencies, 58–59
  analysis of, 55–56
  business conventions, 61
  competition, 61
  dealers and distributors, 58, 63
  evaluating and using, 64–66
  external sources, 61–62
  internal sources
    company records, 57
    employees, 56–57
  obtaining, 62–64
  publications, 61
  retailers, 60, 64
  semicommitted sources, 57–61
  sources of, 55–62
    internal, 56–57
  suppliers, 59–60
  trade associations, 61, 63
Market research, 146
Materials
  bill of materials, 73, 143
  direct materials costs, 42
  specifications, 73–74
Mathematical simulation, 124
Mathematical techniques for solving business problems, 121–25
  operations research; *see* Operations research
  use of probability, 121–22

Net loss, 146
Net profit, 146
Net worth, 146
New products, 50, 57
  financing plan, 100

planning, 29
research, 43

Obsolescence, 146
Oil refinery operations, 123, 125
Operating budgets, 25, 26, 28
Operations, scheduling, 123
Operations research
  aims of, 121
  contributions of, 120
  for decision-making, 120
  defining and identifying problem, 120
  impact on managerial information, 125
  mathematical models or formulas, 121, 124–25
  mathematical simulation, 124
  mathematical techniques for solving business problems, 120
  for military operations, 120
  plant operations scheduling, 123
  probability, use of, 121–22
  typical applications, 121–22
    best routes for traveling salesmen, 122
    distributing products from factories to warehouses and customers, 122
    inventory control, 121–22
    mathematical model of a company, 124–25
    plant operations scheduling, 123
    predicting required number of employees, 122
    research and development, 123–24
  weaknesses of technique, 124
Orders
  analysis, 72
  entry process, 72
  inventory compared with unfilled, 12
  on hand, 71–72
  undelivered, 9
Organization chart, 146
Organizational structure, 108–09
  chain of command, 108–09
  coordination of interdepartmental activities, 114
  delegation and control, 101–10
  effect of computers, 114–17

Overhead, 146
    costs, 36, 42

Packaging, 54
Part and material specifications
    catalogs, 73–74
    inventories, 69
    lists of, 73–74
    material specifications, 73–74
Pension and profit-sharing plans, 87
PERT techniques, 130
PERT/COST techniques, 130
Planning, Programming, Budgeting
    System (PPBS), 128–30
    evaluation of intangible programs,
    130
    identification and allocation prob-
    lems, 129
    use by government agencies, 128–
    30
Plans and planning
    alternative choices, 24–29
    answers question "Where am I
    heading?" 19–20, 30
    balance sheet, 25
    budgets, 25; see also Budgets and
    budgeting
    complications, 28–29
    continuing process, 25–28
    emphasis on in decision making,
    126–30
    identification of alternatives, 127
    impact of, 126
    information on future trends,
    126–27
    entrepreneurial factors, 22–23
    evaluation of whole programs, 127
    executive participation, 24
    external factors, 22–23
    flow charts, 25–26
    goals, 20–21
    importance of, 19
    information required, 24, 26, 29–30
    internal factors, 22–23
    long-range plans, 25, 126
    monthly reports, 25
    motivation for, 5–6
    new products, 29
    "on-the-fly" planning, 21–22
    performance evaluation, 127
    Planning, Programming, Budgeting
    System (PPBS), 128–30
    planning cycle, 126–27

process of review and revision, 27–
    29
production schedules, 74
profit and loss statement, 25
profitability of proposed invest-
    ments, 29
projections, 25
purpose of, 22
selecting course of action, 20–21
time required, 24, 27
top-level strategic, 51
value of, 20
Prices and pricing, 49
    analysis of changes, 56
    based on cost and profit informa-
    tion, 49
    costs, profits, and, 31–51
Product analysis, 146
Product-line decisions, 50
Production
    capacity of equipment, 74
    control system, 79, 146
    customer requirements, 74
    forecasts, 70–71
    inventory management and, 78–79
    lead times, 80
    orders-on-hand, 71–72
    part and material specifications, 73–
    74
    schedules, 74
    use of computers, 116
Products
    market and product information,
    53–62
    evaluating and using, 64–66
    external sources, 61–62
    internal sources, 56–57
    semicommitted sources, 57–61
Profit and loss statements, 34, 47, 146
    projections, 25
Profits
    comparisons of sales to net and
    gross profit, 12
    and cost analyses; see Cost and
    profit analyses
    costs, prices, and, 31–51
    declining profit problem, 31–34
    gross profit for major products, 47
    maximization, 50
    predictions under varying condi-
    tions, 44–47
    special cost and profit analyses, 34–
    38

Profits (*Continued*)
   statements of net and gross profits, 47
   variances with volume, 38–39
Projections
   cash flow, 86
   profit and loss statement, 25
Purchase orders, 80
Purchasing, 96
   inventory management and, 79–81
Purchasing agents, 56, 57

Quality control, 146
Quarterly Financial Report of Manufacturing Corporations, The, 15

Ratios
   comparisons of current liabilities and assets, 12
   comparisons of sales to net and gross profit, 12
   current, 146
Raw materials, inventories, 68, 70
Records
   analysis and summarization, 115
   inventory, 75
   marketing information available in, 56
   reliability of, 8–9
   statistical analysis of, 56–57
Reliability of information, 8–9
   margin of error, 8
Reports
   cost and profit analyses, 34–38
   on costs, prices, and profits, 47
   inventory, 75
   presentation of data, 136–37
   trade associations, 15
Research and development, 36
   operations research technique, 123–24
Retailers
   obtaining information from, 60, 64
   source of information, 60
Retained earnings, 34
Return on investment, 147
Revenue, 147
Risks, calculated, 124

Sales
   analysis of records, 56
   bases of comparison for information, 17

classifications of, 47–48
commissions, 42, 46
forecast, 147
inventory management and, 81–82
market versus product approach, 53–55
by products, 34
selling expenses, 34
static sales-curve problems, 52–55
Sales manager, 62
Salesmen, obtaining market and product information from, 56–57
Securities and Exchange Commission
   The Quarterly Financial Report of Manufacturing Corporations, 15

Services, technical, 60, 65
Simulation, mathematical, 124
Small businesses, use of computers, 118
Space programs
   planning techniques, 126
   PPBS techniques, 129
Specifications, part and material, 73–74
Standardization, 147
Statement of account, 147
Statement of costs and expenses, 47
Statement of manufacturing, selling, and administrative expenses, 47
Statement of net and gross profits
   by channels of distribution, 47
   by customers, 47
   by identifiable divisions of the company, 47
   by major product or product lines, 47
Statement Studies (Robert Morris Associates), 15
Suppliers
   credit terms given by, 98
   obtaining information from, 59–60, 63
Surplus, 147
Systems and methods, 8

Taxes, real estate, 43
Technical support, 60, 65
Time periods, selection of appropriate, 13
Timeliness of information, 9–10

Trade associations
   information available from, 15
   market and product information,
      61, 63
   reports of, 15
Trends, comparisons to indicate, 13

Unit production costs, 5

Variance, definition, 147
Volume of business
   profit variances with, 38–39
   relationship of price, volume, and
      profits, 50

Warehouses, comparisons between, 15
Work in progress, 68